To: Je

with Much Love

Elizabeth

AS I LOOK HOMEWARD

AS I LOOK HOMEWARD

Elizabeth Mosun Wine

Book Guild Publishing
Sussex, England

First published in Great Britain in 2009 by
The Book Guild Ltd
Pavilion View
19 New Road
Brighton, BN1 1UF

Typesetting in Times by
Keyboard Services, Luton, Bedfordshire

Printed in Great Britain by
CPI Antony Rowe

A catalogue record for this book is available from
The British Library

ISBN 978 1 84624 276 2

In memory of my Father, Mr Michael Adeyemi Abiodun and my Grandmother, Mrs Abigail Tolani Aiyelahin Aborisade.

I dedicate this book to my children, Rebecca and Joseph Wine. Thank you for putting up with me while I wrote this book. I love you so much.

Acknowledgements

I thank my editor, Peter Cowlam, for his brilliant work on the book, and Book Guild's Joanna Bentley for her patience with me and a job well done.

I thank my best friend, Belinda Igoni, for her constant support, and my mother-in-law, Mrs Yetta Wine, for her moral support over the years.

Chapter One

I was born on the 12 November 1957 in a village called Mopa, near Kabba, in Nigeria's Kogi State. When I was old enough to do so, I asked my mother what day of the week I had come into the world. She told me she had gone into labour late on the Sunday evening, and that I eventually arrived on the Monday, in the morning. I also learned I always smiled as a baby, and she'd had a lot of fun and pleasure looking after me. Everyone wanted to pick me up and cuddle me.

I was named Elizabeth Mosunmola Abidemi Iyabode Abiodun, and my earliest memory is of the bond or relationship between my mother and me. I wasn't christened, my father not believing in that. My story begins with my great-grandparents' generation, and the special familiarity I enjoyed with my great-grandmother, and my great-grandfather – Ma Ruth and Pa Joshua Aiyelayin. The name Aiyelayin, in Mopa dialect – and probably in the Yoruba language too – means 'there is life after death'. For them there was certainly life *before* death, as they were very much in love with each other.

My grandmother, with the help of her father – my great-grandfather Joshua Aiyelayin – aided the missionaries who had come at the end of the nineteenth century, spreading the gospel and destroying all the traditional worshippers'

1

shrines. Joshua was rewarded with a bicycle, which made him the first person to own one in the whole of the local government authority. My late great-uncle, Ernest Aiyelayin, was rewarded with a lorry. He owned a local cattle ranch, and a cocoa plantation, from which he exported produce to Ghana and various parts of Nigeria. This made him a very prominent man, and it enabled my great-aunt Lydia to attend a private school in Abeokuta, in the Western States of Nigeria – now known as Ogun State – in order to learn to read and write. My grandmother, Madam Abigeal, worked with the missionaries, helping to run the local dispensary. She had no formal training for this, but through experience became as good and efficient as a trained midwife. Of course, all these were somewhat before my time.

I remember one particular sunny day under a huge tree, with beautiful red flowers, as clearly as if it were yesterday. My mother, grandmother and I had walked through Mopa marketplace, and were resting in its shade. My mother and I had travelled two or three days previously from Kano, in the Northern States of Nigeria, where we lived as a family – my father and mother, myself and my younger sister (for six months or more my older brother had being living with my grandfather). My grandmother struck out from the tree and asked the price of a pair of sandals intended for me, trying hard all the time to distract my attention from my mother, who was now boarding a bus to take her back to Kano. I was four years old.

Mopa is divided into north and south, and is called Ileteju and Odole. The reason for this is that all the inhabitants lived in the mountains or up in the hills, which were called Ori-Oke. In both Mopa dialect and in the Yoruba language this translates to 'on the mountains'. In time these same inhabitants were advised or perhaps even forced to move down by the missionaries, because supposedly this was a better or a more civilised way of life. My great-grandparents were married in the mountains. My mother's community and her descendants lived in Ileteju, which is in the north of the village. My grandparents lived just five minutes' walk from my great-grandmother's house, my great-grandfather Pa Joshua Aiyelayin having died a few years after my older brother Debo was born. This was in 1955, when he had reached the age of seventy.

Each community was one extended family, and lived in the same compound. When people got married they would remain living close to their families, so everyone tended to help each other, and almost everyone knew one another. I quite liked the system because in a practical sense it made life less stressful, and socially much more interesting.

My grandmother lived in the missionaries' quarters at the dispensary. It was called Ogba Oyinbo, meaning 'quarters for the white people'. She remained there until she retired in the mid-1960s. She went every other day to visit her mother, all the extended families, and her husband – my grandfather, Pa Nathaniel Aborisade, whose name means 'a child that comes from the gods'. She prepared his food, and mostly got someone to take it to him. Everyone was frightened of her because she was so strict.

My grandfather, too, visited as often as he could, but it was my grandmother who was renowned for her discipline and her very loud voice. I loved her very much and felt at ease with her more so than with him, and I know she had a great and genuine love for me. I owe her my self-discipline, my independence, and many of the principles I have carried forward in my life. Nevertheless, when I was living with her, there was no day that passed when I didn't wish that I was living with my mother and father.

She sometimes worked shifts, which meant delivering babies and circumcising them at any time through the night. Then I would have a babysitter, always a relative. Nevertheless, I would cry myself to sleep, and often wet the bed, a problem that persisted for quite some time. My grandmother was very concerned about this, and got into the habit of waking me in the night to empty my bladder whenever she didn't work the shift. She tried her best.

Usually, before I went to bed – almost every day at 6 p.m. – I made up little songs on my own. I cannot now remember their tunes, but some of the words I can recall:

I am five years old
And I was born in a town called Mopa.
I was taken to Egbe,
I was taken to Kano,
And I was taken to Mopa again.
I do not belong in Mopa.
One day I will go to where I belong,
Which is with my mother and father.

Egbe was my father's town. I carried on singing my song every day at 6 p.m. behind the back of our house at the dispensary. I stopped when I started going to kindergarten.

As I look back, and think of my own seven-year-old son

– of his fondness for wildlife, particularly insects and reptiles – I just know how much he'd have enjoyed the variety of life that I took for granted at the missionaries' quarters. For me it was the most frightening experience. Sometimes, when alone in the little room, I would see a very long grass snake crawling to the wall, and I would scream and rush out. Once I actually saw a snake in the bedroom, and on another occasion a cobra coming towards me when I was playing in the bush in front of our house. That was before the bush was burnt down. Sometimes, I even saw snakes under the pillows of the newly born babies, when the mothers would stop the men who tried to kill them, protesting that the snakes were there to bid a friendly welcome to the world's newest babes. This was all down to their superstitions. I would watch carefully to see if the snakes would do any harm, but they never did, though I was told that in the past many of my distant relatives had been killed by snakebites. My great-aunt Lydia told me that she had lost one of her daughters in this way many years before I was born. And my grandmother, in the course of her life, suffered snakebites three times. In those days there were no proper treatments.

We also had noisy frogs at night, some beautiful singing birds, some nasty eagles who picked little chicks and ate them, some interesting insects, and lots of fruit on the trees. We always picked fruit at any time we liked, when in the ripping season.

All this happened in the early 1960s, though nowadays Mopa is what you'd call modern, as was certainly the case the last time I visited the town, which was in 1989. It was larger than before, with the missionaries very few or hardly there at all. But to return to my story...

As I have said, my grandmother went to the family house every other day to pay everyone a visit, and I went along too. Then I got the chance to see my older brother, who lived officially with my grandfather. This was a typical arrangement for males, and in his case it was so that he could help on the farm. I always thought he lived a much tougher life than I did. I also got the chance to mix and play with my cousins – these were my first and second cousins – and numerous friends from the village, with whom I later went to kindergarten and primary school. We played all sorts of games, mostly with mud and stones, while my grandmother, my great-grandmother and great-aunts, and all sorts of other relatives, chatted and ate away.

Everyone seemed to surround me, except my mother and father. When we weren't playing with mud and stones we preferred pretend cooking, pretend weddings, pretend husbands and wives. This went on in the backyard sometimes, where there were pigs, goats and chickens – in fact, you name it, it was there! One story I have told my family many, many times was when my friends and I saw, at the back of the house, what looked like a very big lump of wood, which we started to handle – until, that is, it turned out to be a python, curled up and asleep! Thankfully it didn't harm us, and was later killed and made into a meal.

All sorts of other things went on. My second cousin once exposed his body to me and wanted me to have sex with him, referring to me as his wife. I was six years old, and fully dressed. I didn't respond, knowing intuitively there was something wrong about this. Nobody had ever told me about sex, or the facts of life. I didn't tell my grandmother about this incident, for fear of a flogging, and her not believing my side of the story. But it remained in my memory, and all I felt was anger towards my mother for sending me to live with my grandmother, and for exposing me to these things at such an early age. I believe that children should remain innocent and kept from such things until they are old enough to manage their emotions.

When we went back to the dispensary, sometimes my older brother came with us. I always liked it when he did, though he was more interested in climbing trees and throwing stones at passers-by. He was always getting into trouble, typical of a lot of boys of his age.

Mopa could get very, very hot in the hot season, and we would all spread our sleeping mats on the verandah at night, which was cooler. I am not too sure if there was anyone with air conditioning in the village at that time, but certainly my grandfather would not have been able to afford it. But it was fun sleeping out. We always told stories to the elders, after they had told stories to us. Some of our folk tales were in the Yoruba language – about the tortoise and how wise he was, and many others besides, mostly about animals. Afterwards we prayed and sang songs from a hymnbook, and we slept.

My grandmother worked hard, and enjoyed what she did, though it left me very lonely. I would play with the patients, the mothers of the newborn babies, and if my older brother Debo sometimes stayed with us, I played with him too. Debo was gifted in reading people's palms, so, when my grandmother was at work during the daytime, this was a facility he offered to the mothers. Most of the time his readings were right, so they all believed in his special powers.

Some of my experiences while living with my grandmother

are quite unforgettable. I remember one day I took and ate some smoked fish without asking permission. She believed I had stolen it, and so punished me severely. She flogged me hard on my thighs and applied chilli peppers on the fresh wounds. You wouldn't believe how painful this was. People around her pleaded for her to stop, but she carried on regardless. I cried for hours and hours until I fell asleep. I still have a big scar on my thighs, which I repeatedly show to my own children. Another bad experience was when one of the patients alleged that my grandmother was always shouting at her, for no reason, and it got to the stage where this patient retaliated by punishing me. She gave me a poisoned orange cut into two halves, which I ate, and became so ill that I lost consciousness. I was rushed to Egbe Hospital, in my father's town nearby – the nearest specialist hospital to us. When I regained consciousness there were drips everywhere, with my nose and throat attached to tubes. My stomach had been pumped. Happily, who should be standing there but my father, who must have just come from Kano to Mopa to visit my brother and me. What a coincidence, I thought.

My father did not take this poisoning lightly at all. He threatened to take whoever was responsible to court. Debo helped to identify the suspect, as I couldn't remember anything myself. The suspect confessed to attempting to kill me because of my grandmother's attitude towards her. At this my grandmother felt so guilty she took all the blame on herself. I was given much attention from all at the dispensary, as well as from my father and grandmother. I felt sorry for her, for now my father suggested I should come back to live with him and my mother. He was still very angry, and said it had never been his idea in the first place for me to live with my grandmother – it had been my mother's. I began to see the picture. I thought that maybe, just maybe, my parents didn't like me enough – not as they liked my sister – and that was why I lived with my grandmother and not with them.

Chapter Two

When I first started at the local kindergarten at our church (the Evangelical Church of West Africa, or ECWA), I was not too keen. I cried every morning when my grandmother walked me there. The first few days I slept throughout the lessons and wet myself again, so that when I woke up I was very embarrassed. We learnt mainly about God and the Bible stories, and recited various psalms. Psalms I liked, and I had three favourites I loved to recite. I couldn't read or write at this time, but I could learn by rote, and was word-perfect with Psalm Ninety-One. This used to make my grandmother and all the teachers happy.

He that dwelleth in the secret place of the most High
Shall abide under the shadow of the Almighty...

During playtime, my friends and I would go to the stream behind the church, throwing things into the water or just messing around. Once, when I was with Mode Orimolade and Bosede Fajemiyo, I slipped and fell into the stream. I was so frightened – I thought I was going to die. They tried to get me out but couldn't, so I had to think for myself. I held on to one of the many rocks in the stream, by this time very deep in the water – all the more alarming, as I was unable to swim. But I was lucky, and found a way out

11

climbing over the rocks and crawling to the bank, where my friends dragged me out completely. Soaking wet as I was, I thought God must have protected me. I went back home with my two companions, where we explained to my grandmother what had happened. I was terrified of how she would react, but rather than the flogging I half expected, she let me off, so I got away with that one.

On Sundays, we attended church services three times. There was Sunday school for children, and the morning and evening services. At Sunday school we learnt more Bible stories, sang songs, acted out plays and performed Bible readings. This was more exciting for us than the main service, whose sharp division was between the choir and the rest of the congregation. The choir mostly sang songs of praise written by the choirmaster. The ECWA was well known for its beautiful music, so much so that they had a broadcast radio station based in Liberia, West Africa. Their music went out to most of the West African countries every Sunday afternoon. I recited poems from the Bible, sang in the church and took part in a lot of Bible story dramatisations, such as Joseph and his many-coloured coat. The church congregation would applaud enthusiastically, with my grandmother, her friends, my great-grandmother, some of my cousins and the whole family there in attendance. I will forever love those songs the choir always sang.

Sunday was a very special day in the village, with both young and old wearing their best attire. It was very colourful. The minister and his wife would ring the bell for the morning service at 10 a.m., and for the evening service at 4 p.m. The Christians and all the churchgoers of the village got excited and went off to church in joyous mood. There were, too, many activities after the church service, with light refreshments and sometimes proper meals prepared by my grandmother and her sisters-in-law, a task they alternated with others the following Sunday.

At the age of six I started my primary education, at Arungbo Mission School, which was one of two main schools in the village. The other was run by the local government authority, though at ours we paid school fees. In those days just about everything was colonised – or almost colonised – even though Nigeria had just won independence from the British. The standard of education and facilities were very different from when I came to live in England.

Going to school was not something I used to look forward to. I still had many friends, whom I regarded as *good* friends, because they continued to call at my family house to ask my mother to send me their love. Some of these I call on still whenever I visit Nigeria.

I did like my friends, and I enjoyed playing with them. If not for anything else, they liked to play with my toys, especially my different baby dolls, which were mostly given to me by my grandmother's boss, and by my father. I took one of my dolls everywhere – to school, to church, to my great-grandmother's house. I put it on my back and tied it with a piece of cloth. I got the nickname Mosun Oni Baby, which means Mosun the baby carrier, an epithet conferred on me by the other children and their mums. I have since given my favourite baby doll to my daughter, but I don't think she's that keen on it. Of more interest to her are Barbie and Sindy.

After school I sold kerosene in bottles, under the same big tree with the beautiful red flowers in the marketplace where I had been parted from my mother. I had friends who did this with me, with all of us in it for the fun. Other friends I knew, who were less fortunate than me, did jobs like this out of necessity. I saved money from the work I did, always intending to put it to good use. When my grandmother called an end to this job, I began to consider all I had put by in my moneybox. She asked me what I would like to spend it on. When I told her she took me to the market, where I bought three different pieces of material. They were sewn into what became my first Nigerian traditional outfit. And, as I was always dressed smartly, my grandmother took a lovely photograph, and named the attire Iro and Buba.

My aunt Tinus's daughter, my cousin Funmilayo, who was about two or three years younger than me, lived with my great-aunt Dada (better known as Mama Sunday) and her husband, the late Pa Balogun. They arrived from Lagos following their retirement, after living there for many years. Funmilayo I saw on weekends. My grandmother and Great-Aunt Dada were always interested to know who had dressed up their grandchildren the best. It must have been fun for them.

Mama Sunday was quiet and gentle, and compared with my grandmother, very softly spoken. She spoilt Funmilayo rotten. Pa Balogun was the strict one. Whenever we visited them he spoke in Yoruba. Having been in Lagos for so long he spoke very little Mopa – in fact, none at all. Funmilayo and I used to giggle when he spoke. I liked him because he would always ask about my welfare and about my schoolwork and how I was getting on.

In one academic year we had three examinations in which I didn't do well. I came second to last in my class. My grandmother blamed the teacher, though between them they worked out a compromise – she now did my homework with me, but only in the subject of Yoruba. She got a friend to help with maths and English. At the end-of-year examination I came second top – a surprise for me and also my parents, when they received the report. My father questioned it and I did question it myself. I had certainly improved, but not that dramatically.

My grandmother prepared special jollof rice and chicken to celebrate. She invited friends to join us, and during the gathering we discovered that the teacher, together with my grandmother, had engineered my position. I don't know if my father ever learned the truth – even years later.

I will never forget one day in school when we were all asked to finish our class work before the midday meal, and told that whoever failed to do so would have to remain in class and forgo lunch. Of course, I did not finish on time, so I was not allowed to go home. As we only lived five minutes from school, my grandmother expected me home, but when I didn't turn up she came in to school herself. My class teacher explained why he had kept me, and knowing her reputation, everyone was frightened of what she might do or say. I sat there anxiously, though in the end was still not allowed to go home for my lunch. My grandmother went back – just across the road – and returned with black-eyed beans cooked with plantain and other ingredients. It was one of her specialities. She marched into the classroom and commanded me to eat it, and naturally I was hugely embarrassed, there in front of all the other children.

It used to be very interesting and exciting at the dispensary, come the mornings. My grandmother led our prayers and read a sermon, then we all sang choruses and hymns, with all the sick people, pregnant women, young mothers and their children gathered with us. It lifted all our spirits. The aim was to combine the spiritual healing, prayers and preaching of Christian worship with the more conventional aspects of that religion. It seemed to work out well, because the reported death rate at the dispensary fell at about that time.

During the school holidays my grandmother and I went to Kaduna in the northern part of Nigeria, to visit my parents who now lived there. I can remember my father complaining at the standard of education I was getting through living with my grandmother. My overall lifestyle also concerned him. In fact there was constant arguing over my welfare. My father would say to my grandmother that he had had enough of my living with her, and that he wanted her to hand me back. He threatened to take drastic action if my grandmother refused to comply with his wishes. My mother always chose to stay quiet over the matter, which filled me with mixed emotions.

My older brother Debo had returned to live with my parents, while my sister Tokunbo lived with them in Kaduna too. My mother had five children, with Tokunbo the only one who made a success of living with my parents in that childhood period. I always enjoyed the holidays in Kaduna, and being with my brother and sister, and I looked up to my father as a role model. He was very smart and intelligent, and not at all shy like my mother. Quite the opposite: he was dynamic, and meant everything in the world to me. In later years, however, there were things I disagreed with him about, though I still found all these qualities in him – an honest man, extremely generous and kind. Conversely, my mother said very little to me throughout the holidays. She assumed everything was all right as far as I was concerned, even living with my grandmother. That said, we always did things together, as it was always a very full house and a very large one, too. We had four live-in helpers. Two of them were my mother's cousins. Then there was my aunt Remi, who had been living with my parents since she was five years old – and she helped out too. She was a favourite of theirs.

In the early evenings at about 5 p.m. my parents would take us to visit their friends, who all occupied high office, such as the then Minister for Education, the late Mr S.A. Ajayi. Another I remember was Alhaji Isa Kathir, also a minister. It was fun for me to observe the protocol, what with the massive and well-decorated government residences. This was quite different from my life in the village.

We would be introduced to the minister and his family, and they would offer us refreshments, after which we were off out to play with his children. My father discussed politics, something he later participated in himself. Also in politics was my mother's uncle, the late Chief Ade-John, then the Permanent Secretary for Education. They lived two doors away from us, and we would be constantly in and out of their house, being sent on errands there. The chief's older boy went to see my aunt Remi a lot, especially when my parents were at work.

Sometimes in the afternoon, my grandmother, my mother, my aunt Remi, my aunt Taiye, my brother, my sister and myself would go to the big market, mainly to buy new clothes.

It was all fun to me, because it was a big city, so different from Mopa. At Kaduna's market everyone spoke in broken English, English proper and the Hausa language. At this time Yoruba was not spoken in the town. I loved all these differences. People in the market had a slightly different complexion and bone structure from ours, which all seemed to make my grandmother all the more hilarious. She would always want to fit in, especially while negotiating for food and other goods in the market, and in fact she spoke the broken English so well that she always came home with a bargain. As I've always said, she got what she wanted every time.

Naturally, we used to buy lots of things to take back to Mopa. I would get all my back-to-school stuff, shoes, and so on.

On Sundays my father, my mother and all the children went for what my father called a ride. This was like an adventure for me. It was a drive from Kaduna to Zaria, or even as far as Kano, in his big Citroën. He would try to overtake all the other cars on the road to Zaria, and showed us just how fast he could go. Indeed he loved his Citroën. It would take us all afternoon, and on the way we would sing so loudly that my father would shout at us to stop, because it was affecting his concentration.

Now it was almost time to go back to Mopa, with our clothes, shoes and money (for our school fees and living expenses). Mostly we would travel by train for half of the journey, with the other half by bus or lorry, while my siblings got driven in luxurious cars, and sometimes even had their own drivers for school and other journeys. Although *I* always had mixed emotions about this, my grandmother was always happy to be back with me at Mopa. I wished I lived with my parents, but at the same time felt sorry for my grandmother, who wanted so much for me to live with her. All her friends and family would come to welcome us back, and we would bring presents for almost all of them. My grandmother's boss was also happy to see us back, because she virtually ran the dispensary and the people took to her. She was also responsible for cooking for Miss Baker, one of the medical workers from the white missionary. Some of the missionaries had been given Yoruba names by the locals. One was named Bankedun, and another Folorunsho. I always thought Bankedun was pompous.

Miss Baker was English, and Bankedun and Folorunsho were Canadians. Folorunsho left Nigeria for Canada in the mid-1960s, for good. Quite a few people travelled all the way to Apapa, Lagos, to see her off at Apapa Wharf, where she sailed away by ship. There were floods of tears, most especially from my grandmother, though not from me. Miss Baker left for England in the mid-1970s, just when I was beginning to think she would stay in Nigeria for the rest of her life. She was very much loved by the people of Mopa.

My grandmother adored Folorunsho – she was her favourite boss. She was very loyal to her, and they wrote to each other many, many years after she had left for Canada. She also spoke Yoruba. My grandmother always asked if I had ever come across Folorunsho in London, and I always had to explain that London is a long way from Canada.

Chapter Three

In Mopan culture, the people celebrated festivals and worshipped many gods. Before I go further into this, I would like to stress that no offence is intended to any religion. What we call 'oriki' is the title given to each community of extended families. My oriki is 'the Iyajagans', where we have been converted to Christianity. For that reason I am forbidden from taking part in these celebrations or worshipping their idols. My orikis are Iyajagan and the Omoee. They were inherited through my mother's mother – my grandmother's line, via Madam Abigeal Tolani Aborisade's family. In Mopa dialect, the orikis, which are chanted, go like this:

1. Iyajagan – Omo gan ran gan ran ijobi
2. Omo Iyagba I dare ewa nghun
3. Oun jagan
4. Aboyun e ro bo idire
5. Ho oko m
6. Omoee age
7. Ho omoee
8. Ho oko m

In Egbe, my father's hometown (Micah Abiodun), the orikis go like this:

1. Oun soko
2. Oun sara (la poto)
3. Oun yem
4. Okun iyem

These orikis are forms of praise, usually of your children, in the mornings, or whenever they do anything substantial and good, or achieve a high standard in anything. They are supposed to make your head swell and the hair on the back of your neck stand up, and generally show how much love you have for all your children. They are passed down from generation to generation. My grandmother Abigeal showered me with all these orikis, as did my father's sister (my aunt Mama Agbe). All these praises, this chanting of orikis, early in the morning when I knelt down to say good morning – especially from my grandmother Abigeal – went on until I left Nigeria for England, and whenever I went on holiday back to Nigeria.

The cultural and traditional people of Mopa worshipped some of the following gods: the Imole, the Sango, the Oro, the Oshun and the Orisa or Orisha, and took part in the Egungun festivals. The Imole worshippers strongly believed in their gods. They put on exotic shows and dances. They wore white costumes and a great many colourful beads. They could get into quite a procession during their dancing, but they soon calmed down. They also claimed to be possessed by demons. Everyone was allowed to watch them during their festival, but not necessarily join in.

I do not remember what the Imole god symbolised, but Sango was a god of lightning and thunder, and was widely worshipped in the whole of Yorubaland, the Iyagba area that included Mopa. Oro was a god worshipped by men only during ceremonies. They had strict and highly dangerous rules. When the Oro worshippers dressed in their ceremonial costumes, and during festivals, they marched from one end of the town to the other, performing their rituals. No women were allowed to walk on the street or come out during the hours they paraded. People were not allowed to see them perform their rituals except if you were one of them. In the dark ages, any woman who accidentally came out, or peeped, was taken and instantly killed. As the years went by, and as the rules became less inflexible, women who accidentally watched them were cursed, a practice that still persists to this day. Oshun was a god of water, mostly worshipped in Yorubaland.

Egungun was a masquerade, and a very popular one, involving extremely beautiful costumes. I once joined in an Egungun festival during the parade, without letting my grandmother know. Egungun was used to worship other gods, and this was widely the case in most black countries all over the world. People – especially children – dressed up to raise money for causes. I have seen these beautiful masquerades reproduced here in the Notting Hill carnival in London. The only difference between them is that here in the UK there are no ritual sacrifices of goats or chickens.

My grandmother had a friend, Iyagbale, who was the leader of the Imole worshippers. I guessed they grew up together. She always dressed in her costumes. She called round to the house whenever my grandmother went to visit her mother, not being welcome at the dispensary where my grandmother lived. They would argue incessantly as to what their various gods meant to them. My grandmother quoted verses from the Bible, while Iyagbale would recite rituals and dance. Mostly they parted without resolving their argument. My great-grandmother, usually, did not get involved in these exchanges and only smiled instead. I looked on with interest.

Around the Mopa dispensary, as I said earlier, there were many different fruits and flowers. We ate a lot of these fruits, and some were made into wine. People, including children, would come to pluck at the fruit, or hurl stones up to dislodge it. Where the rest of the extended family lived, including my great-aunt Lydia, it was usual to make red corn and millet into a wine called burukutu. This I loved to drink – though too much was intoxicating. My great-aunt Lydia drank so much burukutu and palm wine over the years that she was drunk a lot of the time. My great-grandmother complained about it bitterly, this being a great worry for her.

Performing Efon Ceremonies in Egbe Town

Efon is a ceremony performed by females from age twelve to young adulthood. Only certain women from each compound's various communities are entitled to perform the ceremony. Some, and not all families in Egbe, are privileged to carry out this performance, for which I do not know the reason – something, I suspect, deeply rooted in tradition.

The ceremony is a rite-of-passage preparation towards adulthood, designed to open all future areas of life, particularly concerning marriage (as it is normally performed before betrothal). Mostly the woman in question already has a suitor in mind, and the ceremony coincides with that period preceding the payment of a dowry. No marriage is recognised – and this is still true today – without either the process of Efon or the appropriate payment, which demands the giving of goats, chickens, pigs, kola nuts, palm oil and a monetary levy. This is requested by the elders of the community. It is said that where the performance of Efon is omitted, misfortune will befall the woman. The venue for the ceremony is made safe by the organisers and through family mediations, and the performance itself requires years of practice by the ladies. Women look forward to it, some for the prestige of it, some for the sheer enjoyment, and others for the initiation itself.

Girls or young women carry out the ceremony by carrying calabashes on their heads filled with fruits and other delicacies. They wear short traditional skirts and very small blouses, revealing very little, but not usually covering their stomachs. They all have the same traditional hairdo, and walk in straight lines, very slowly, not talking or singing to each other. They walk from one end of the town to the other, where the venue is situated, and prior to the journey they will have been at a gathering in one of the big houses, for several days, eating and drinking (though not alcohol). The idea is to encourage familiarity with each other.

The venue is also a big house, with a compound, with its whereabouts kept a secret right to the last moment, its location a secluded one in Odo Egbe, in a quarter of the town always used for this purpose. What goes on inside the house is supervised and controlled by the organisers of the ceremony, and it is well known that no man is allowed in or near or within a given radius of the house at this critical time. The women are meant to emerge from the house healthier and plumper than when they went in – and that's the reason for so much rich food.

Stories told to those who have not yet participated in the ceremony involve women given whole chickens to themselves to eat in a single day, with lots of traditional Egbe accompaniments besides. The women have many tasks individually assigned to them. They learn about married life and traditional values. They dance traditional dances, interacting with each other, and are counselled by their supervisors, who are mostly traditional herbalist and medicine women. They also bathe in a cold shallow pond each day. They remain at the venue for a month, that being the length of time tradition dictates for the ceremony. The parents, especially the mothers at home, tend to show off, telling all their friends that their daughters have gone for Efon.

In latter years, due to the influence of Christian evangelism, the tradition has been called into question, not least for the cost involved. The vast number of people now travelling and living in bigger cities, and even abroad, and with that, the inevitable dilution of the meaning and aim of Efon has also to be considered. Women can enter into marriage without the ceremony having been performed, yet community elders will still add a fee to the dowry, which it is considered vital to pay.

I am one of those women qualified to take part in Efon. I have not done this yet. The elders are still waiting for me to pay the fee and perform the ceremony. One day I will pay the fee, though I have no intention of participating in the ceremony.

*   *   *

It could be fun sometimes in Mopa, because we had various Nigerian artists, comedians and dancers coming to perform at the house of one of my grandmother's family friends, a man named Mr Ronke. He ran part of his house as a nightclub. His wife was a good friend of mine too. Many times we had famous artists such as the late Herbert Ogunde playing there. I was privileged to meet and watch him perform, and all for free! I was even asked to perform on stage with him once, which I did. A lady comedian called Baby Ranco also often performed at the nightclub.

I was shocked one day in 1992 when I was in a corner shop near where I live in England. The shopkeeper asked me what country I came from, and when I said Nigeria she asked if I knew Herbert Ogunde, who had recently died. I was aghast and sad and knew I would miss him. He had the most beautiful voice and was a good entertainer. The shopkeeper and her husband used to know him personally as well.

But back to 1965. My mother was about to have another baby, my sister Titilola, in Kaduna. My grandmother and I went there. I didn't know what the discussion or decision made about me by my parents and grandmother was, but I knew I didn't have a long time to stay in Mopa. No one consulted me about this.

One afternoon, a man arrived from Kaduna. He was a family friend of my parents, and was the vicar of the church where they worshipped. He was the late Reverend Olusiyi. He came with a letter from my father, which said that when the reverend returned to Kaduna I should definitely go back with him. Oh my God! My grandmother was so downhearted, and *I* had my mixed feelings again. This was all so very

27

sudden, and I was leaving Mopa at last. I consoled myself during the long train ride from Ilorin to Kaduna, where the tropical scenery had me transfixed. For the leg to Ilorin I travelled with both the reverend and my grandmother, then went on to Kaduna alone by surface train. There were floods of tears from both my grandmother and me when she saw me off at last. I missed her so much when I got to Kaduna, and for a long time I would not socialise.

My father tried very hard to see that I got on with my sister Tokunbo. He also did his best to improve my educational standard. He got my older brother Debo and me a private tutor, whom we called Uncle Sunday. Uncle Sunday came in the early evening three times a week. He assured my father there was potential in me, and that I was doing much better than my brother.

It was a holiday period when I arrived, but the time I spent there went quickly. I started at the same school as Tokunbo, until places for me and my brother were found in the nearby town of Zaria. Tokunbo and I were at the same school for two terms, after which I boarded at St Bartholomew's, Wusasa, in Zaria. I was nearly eight years old. I didn't feel comfortable, and I didn't have a proper education either, largely because I didn't concentrate in class, a consequence of not being happy. The routine was not relaxed enough for me – in fact, it was all too tough in every respect.

One of our pastimes in the evening usually took place alongside our large kitchen, where we would queue up to buy *fura de no no*. *Fura de no no* is a traditional food of the northerners. It is made mostly of yogurt and milk, drunk with millet dough from a special recipe. All Hausa people crave for it and it sells like hot cakes around dinner or supper time. My father was a special customer of one lady called Miss Tabrini and they would always flirt together while all the adults or the housemaids were preparing supper. *Fura de no no* has a special selling song, which goes like this: *'Fura de no no. De ge de hey'*.

There was a coup d'état in Nigeria in 1966, and soon afterwards the Nigerian civil war broke out. My brother Adebowale (Debo) and I were still in Zaria, leaving only a year later, and my parents still lived in Kaduna. Significantly, St Bartholomew's was a private boarding school well known for admitting mostly the children of top politicians or government officials. My father had a prominent and stable career as a teaching principal, active politician and adviser to Sir Ahmadu Bello, the Sardauna of Sokoto, late Premier of the Northern State of Nigeria. He was summoned often to Ahmadu Bello, the Sardauna of Sokoto's residence (simply called Sardauna). They discussed politics and administration, things I was too young to understand. All I could say of Sir Ahmadu Bello was that he had many wives. He called my father his 'boy', being much younger than he was. He was fond of him and admired his ability and intelligence, and used him for much of his administrative work, for his advice and for his mastery of English. Sometimes my father wrote his speeches.

On 15 January 1966 the first coup d'état happened in Nigeria. I remember the day that Sardauna, of Sokoto, was killed, as I do the day the same thing happened to Sir Abubakar Tafawa Balewa, the first Prime Minister of the Federal Democratic Republic of Nigeria. It was a very sad moment in our house – number 44 BZ Sardauna Crescent, Kaduna. It was as if my father had lost a relation. I had never seen him so distraught and sad. He did not eat, and he panicked and went into hiding. No one in our household ventured out for several days, for fear of being tortured by the soldiers, who would know my father's connection with Sardauna. By now all the top politicians had been killed, including Chief Akintola, the Premier of the Western State. Top civil servants too had perished, many of them known to my parents, and regular visitors to our house.

The late Agunyi Ironsi of the Eastern State of Nigeria became the first temporary Military Head of State of Nigeria, and it was chaos in the whole of the country at that time. My father gradually came out more and drove into town. He was searched often by soldiers on patrol, just like any other politician or top civil servant of that era. On more than one occasion he was ordered by soldiers to stand on top of his car and put his two hands above his head while he was searched. This was intentional humiliation, showing they suspected him of belonging to the old regime, which of course was true. It was a fearful time for almost everyone, and certainly for me and my family. Massacre followed, looting and killing of innocent people, some of whom we'd known as friends. I do not want to go into the details of all the atrocities that then took place; it is all too painful for me, even now.

Justina Nwachukwu was one of my childhood friends, and was at the St Joseph Nursery Primary School in Kaduna. She came from Onisha in the Eastern State of Nigeria. We parted shortly before the war because the Ibo people were ordered to leave wherever they were and go back to their place of birth. This was because the war was between the Nigerian government and the Biafran people from the Eastern

State of Nigeria. Justina and her family left, and we have never heard from each other since. I do not know if she is dead or alive to this day. I always pray for a miracle to happen, and that we can see each other one day. War is a devastating blight on humanity.

Everyone talks about what they were doing on the day the Nigerian civil war broke out. My oldest brother, Theophelous Folrunsho Abiodun – my half-brother, my father's first child – told me he was on his way to his first interview for work.

Soon my father was transferred to work in another town, Oturpko, which was not too far from the war front. He was a teacher, the head of a college that trained people to be administrators. Part of his work was touring other schools in the area, as a peripatetic. He was usually away from home for a week at a time. My mother was a nurse and did not immediately go to live with him in Oturpko, as she was unable to get transferred herself. She joined him much later. As a consequence, we all lived with my mother for a short time before we were able to move. We went back to our old school, the St Joseph Catholic Primary School in Kaduna. Living with my mother was just like falling from grace. Tokunbo and I walked to school instead of being taken and collected by car. We lived in a very small house, and played truant a lot. I always used to engineer this, my sister being so reluctant that I always had to threaten her. Almost every day we set off to school, but never arrived. Part of the reason was I was interested in knowing and seeing more of the rural areas in Kaduna, which resulted more often than not in a trek for many miles all over the place.

We sometimes saw my mother during the course of her

work, treating and visiting the sick or patients who lived out in these rural areas. She was a midwife as well as a community nurse, so it was part of her job to get out and about. If we saw her at a distance we would quickly hide, in any available place we could find before she saw us. We tried all sorts of things while roaming the town, and saw lots of strange things too. We had heard from school or were told by other kids that it wasn't unusual for them to eat sand, as it tasted good. I decided to eat some each time we were near a building site, and got my sister to do the same. Amazingly, it did taste good, though we did stop eating it after a while. If we saw something unusual we always returned to the spot, to make sure it was really true, however incredible it seemed. And of course, we made sure we returned home in the early evening just when the schools had closed.

There were very young girls who sold kola nuts and groundnuts from large trays they carried on their heads. As we watched, some two or three old men, sitting on mats on the floor of their house, their windows wide open, seemed to make signals to them. They feigned interest in making a purchase, with the real intent of luring them into their rooms for sex. Extraordinarily, these men were well over seventy. My sister and I were shocked, and always wanted to tell our mother, who'd surely round on these men and shame them for their wrongdoing. But, surprisingly, as soon as these girls had entered the house they took off their clothes without any struggle or coercion. They seemed to look forward to it, which to me and my sister was a puzzle we'd discuss long after lights-out every night at bedtime. These girls were only aged between eight and ten.

We all went to live with my father at Oturpko about six months after he left Kaduna. To help look after us, there were two housemaids and two nannies. It was a big house with lots of trees and fruit: paw-paw, mango, guava. We also had livestock, such as ostriches, ducks, chickens, turkeys and goats. I loved it there and I was happy. Soon I had a crush on a boy called Justin, who was in my class. He was the nephew of the Emir of Idoma. Emirs are traditional Muslim religious rulers, highly placed in society, especially in the Northern State of Nigeria. Justin, my sister and I walked home together after school whenever we were not being fetched. Justin and I stopped in the bushes and kissed each other, sometimes gently on the lips, and sometimes passionately. Naturally, we went with my father to the Emir's palace at any opportunity, which was lots of fun.

Justin was the only boy I had a proper crush on. My sister Toks watched every movement between us, and would tell my father about it unless I promised to stop bullying her. So, we made a deal. I had bullied my sister a lot, though not physically. I used to send her on errands, or make her do my chores, or shout very loudly at her, threatening to cease to be her friend. On the question of friends in general, I had many more than she ever dreamed of. She was a loner, but thankfully I could no longer see myself bullying her, or anyone else for that matter.

After school my older brother Adebowale – or Debo – used to cycle all around the town, ending up at the marketplace, just before dinner. He would use an adult bicycle that belonged to my father. The marketplace was almost five miles from our house. I sometimes cycled with him to the palace gates, Justin being one of Debo's friends. Unfortunately

33

for us, the security men at the gates wouldn't allow us in with our cycles. Perhaps they should have, because cycling at all was a bit of a hazard, what with the many risks we took in traffic. Thankfully we survived, though I think back with horror at how my feet struggled to stay on the pedals securely. I was very small, but with my brother beside me, I felt nothing could go wrong. All this usually went on when my father took his two-hour nap after work. He called it his siesta, and woe betide us if we woke him from it.

He was a little lonely in Oturpko without my mother. He socialised with friends a lot, and played hockey and lawn tennis and went out horse riding, which evidently didn't fill his needs. He married another woman about a year after we got there, being allowed by native law and custom to do so. He and members of his teaching staff tended to have wild parties at the Federal Training Centre, about twice a week, involving all their new young wives and partners. My brothers, sister and I could hear the music, even from the house. My father, with his new wife, and accompanied by a neighbouring couple, would come back very late while we were supposedly in bed asleep, though of course I remained wide awake, curious at all their goings-on, and at how drunk they all were (apart from my father, who never drank).

His method of discipline was flogging. He had special leather canes for that purpose – one for each of us, inscribed with our names. When we did something wrong, the punishment was six or twelve lashes, according to age. Here in Oturkpo was the first time my father had caned me. He now saw me as old enough, and was of the opinion that I had always been spoilt by my grandmother, and now needed firmer discipline. Obviously I disagreed with this, though dared not state that view. Moreover, he had paid a great deal of money to a local craftsman for these leather canes, a point always emphasised by the fact that he would check them where they hung, to ensure they remained intact. My two older brothers were lashed almost every day. Next most frequent was me. Olatokunbo got it a total of two or three times, because she was the youngest.

There was an argument one evening between Debo and me, which turned into an ugly fight. He beat me so unsparingly I was at a loss to know how to defend myself. I bit him so hard on his nipples that they dangled off and were about to detach themselves completely. An ambulance was called and he was taken to the general hospital. I was frightened and worried for him, though he was stitched back together and recovered over time. On his first night back from the hospital I begged him to forgive me – I was genuinely sorry, and thankfully he did forgive me (to the point that we have never talked of this since). My father didn't flog me either, which everyone expected him to do. He weighed all the evidence and because my brother had beaten me up – not just on this occasion, but several times – he gave me a warning only.

Chapter Four

The late Dr Nmandi Azikiwe, the first President of the Federal Republic of Nigeria, and the first lady, Flora Azikiwe, came to visit Oturkpo and all the neighbouring towns. Their itinerary included Markudi. I suppose there were negotiations under way, despite the continuing massacres in places like Kaduna and Kano City. Perhaps by then he was merely a ceremonial head – but of this I'm not sure.

When he and his wife visited us, all we schoolchildren lined the streets, dancing our traditional dances, singing songs and waving the Nigerian flag. He was a very handsome man, I thought, and his wife one of the most elegant people I have ever seen. We children ran alongside the motorcade, all over the town. There was loud music everywhere, especially in the marketplace. One particular piece of music that had just come out at the time was played and sung by the Ibo traders all over town. It was of a kind mostly sung by people from what is now the River State of Nigeria, and it went like this:

Obona bereboane
Obona berebote
Aye-e Obona bereboane,
Obona berebote,
Obona berebote,

Aye-e Obona bereboane
Obona berebote, etc.

It was played loudly all day, with people dancing to it on the streets.

My father, with his friends and colleagues, had been busy with preparations for the president's visit. He knew Zik, as he called him, well from his early contact, as was also the case with the late Chief Obafemi Awolowo, the two of them having been in England at about the same time, at one point sharing an apartment. He told us stories about these two people on many, many occasions. I felt sorry for my father. There he had been, working and studying hard all through his life, but never attaining the great fame these people had. He was, I have to say, never bitter about this. He was kind, good, intelligent, honest, and I valued him for these qualities. For him, a good name was worthier than fame and wealth.

There was another coup d'état, which saw Agunyi Ironsi ousted by the government of Major-General Yakubu Gowon. The war broke out in the May of 1967. Nigerian armed forces were led by Gowon against the Biafran leader, Colonel Odumegwu Ojukwu. We were trained at school to lie down flat as soon as we heard the sound of an aeroplane, or suspected that one flying low in our direction was about to release a bomb. We carried out these exercises while at play at the front of the house when school was over, and sometimes we experienced the real thing, twice missing a bomb.

My grandmother Abigeal came to visit us. She brought my two-year-old sister Titilola, who lived with my mother in Kaduna. She stayed and looked after us, picking us up from school. One day, while on a grassy path, she was bitten by a snake, which she thought nothing of until two or three days later, when her whole body swelled up and she was dizzy all of the time. She was rushed to hospital. When we learned of the bite we were all very surprised. Personally, I was sure it hadn't been a dangerously poisonous snake, because the symptoms had taken two days to manifest themselves, and furthermore, she'd survived.

Later that year my mother moved from Kaduna to live in a town called Oturpka, a twenty-minute drive from us in Oturpko. My aunt Tinuola, my mother's younger sister, was pregnant and came to stay with us for the birth, our hospital facilities being that much better than hers. When it came, the baby was a girl, Adunola. I grew very fond of her, holding her, feeding her and playing a lot. I was young myself and must have seen her as a toy. One bright and breezy morning I woke before Aunt Tinu, and for that matter everyone else in the house. I made up a milk formula in Adunola's bottle and fed her. The next thing I knew she was gasping and her eyes had turned white, then she was unconscious. I was frightened and screamed, and put her on the floor. My grandmother, the bravest among us, took control of the situation, giving first aid before taking her to hospital. Once there her stomach was pumped, and tubes were passed through her nose to drain the excess fluid. The problem was I had given her very hot milk, not having tested its temperature beforehand. She was a mere seven days old.

During that hospitalisation process I ran away from home, and stayed away all day. I dodged through the nearby bushes into the forest to hide. My family searched for me all day, and were very concerned for my safety. I thought that Adunola had died, and I felt so guilty for having killed another human being. In the forest I saw some Nigerian Army armoured cars. They were travelling east, on active duty due to the civil war. The soldiers were armed with machine guns, and looked very scary. They were about to take control of some Biafran towns, Oturkpo and Oturpka being near the Biafran border. I ran quickly, faster and faster into the thick of the forest, in order to avoid their questions, as they were bound to want to know whether I was Biafran or Nigerian. Luckily I escaped this situation, otherwise I might have been killed or taken hostage if they had not believed my story. It was a dangerous time for a child to be on the run, but fortunately I got home safely.

Then something happened at school that frightened us all. One lunchtime we were standing under a big tree, when suddenly there was thunder and a bolt of lightning struck one of my two friends, Ladi. It thrust her up in the air and threw her back down, her body aflame when she landed, while all around was deluged with rain. The school authority called for an ambulance, but before it came, Ladi's father, who was the town chief, enlisted people of traditional beliefs to perform ceremonies on her. They danced around her, casting African magic. My other friend and I thought she was going to die. However, she was eventually taken to hospital, though not before all the magic rites had been carried out. The whole school was in a state of shock, and we were allowed to be collected early. My grandmother came to fetch me, in a frightened state herself, praying all the time that it wasn't me who'd been struck. After two weeks in hospital Ladi recovered. She returned to school later, clearly lucky to be alive, though very badly burnt.

On another occasion at school a boy in my class who

suffered from epilepsy had a serious fit, which threw him into the well. The school was evacuated and the medical team tried to rescue him. Luckily the well was dry, and he survived. We were all sent home and asked to pray for him. Another experience that has remained etched in my mind is the volcano that erupted in Oturpko. It lasted for several days, and mercifully there were no casualties. We could see the lava flow on our way to and from school.

The war had deteriorated further and my father had to send the family away to his hometown of Egbe, in Nigeria's Kogi State. My mother had come to join us, and was here with my father's other wife, though now of course in Egbe we embarked on another new life, just as many other families had. Only my father was left in Oturpko, teaching. We were frightened for him, not knowing what might befall him. The domestic staff came with us, and we travelled through Lokoja in Kogi State, using a large lorry that carried our belongings. I remember the ferry crossing, and how relieved we were on reaching Lokoja, which was not very far from Egbe. Sadly we'd left all our classmates and friends behind, including Justin, but after only a couple of months my father joined us, the war having reached its peak, with all the schools and colleges in Oturpko shut.

We started a new school in Egbe, with me in primary five. Soon we made new friends, many of whom I still see whenever I go to Nigeria on holiday (it is very important for me to do that). I had moved around so much in my young life, but for the first time we were able to live in the same town or village for three to four years at a stretch.

We learnt so much in my new school and I was especially happy with my new friends. We went to church regularly

41

and I soon joined its choir. We practised twice a week, which I always looked forward to, not least because then I missed out on the household chores at teatime. My friends, the twins Taiye and Kehinde Alaya, came to fetch me. They, the late Bosede Koledade and I were known among the choir as the 'foursome', because we were the best of friends. The late teacher Paul, one of my father's childhood friends, was the choirmaster – not only here but also at the Oke-Egbe ECWA church. He composed and wrote most of the songs we choristers sang, and was a very talented man. He was also a good guitarist, and I don't think the ECWA can have had many more professional and able musicians than he was. I still keep my choir book, and when I sing from it, which I often do, I feel nothing but nostalgia.

The 'foursome' were also members of the Girls' Brigade. There were various activities, including camping holidays, which entailed craftwork such as making pots and plates from clay. There was once a camping trip to Mopa – my mother's town – but I did not go because my mother claimed she couldn't afford to pay. I was very disappointed, as all the other girls went. They enjoyed doing lots of creative things, such as painting, embroidery, knitting, and learning how to make a campfire.

Bosede Koledade drank some contaminated water at Okedigba Primary School where they camped. She came back with a disease known as typhoid fever. She was admitted to the SIM, or Sudan Interior Mission hospital, at Egbe (my father's town) for over a week. Taiye and Kehinde and all members of her family saw her every day during visiting hours, though I didn't visit. I wasn't brave enough to face her condition. She was a very courageous girl, and a very

42

religious person too, and hung on for ten days in the hospital before she died. I was told by my friends and her family that before her last breath, Bosede had asked for a reading of her favourite passage from the Holy Bible. She sent good wishes to her brother especially, and to all her close friends, including me.

The whole choir sang at her funeral, except me, and chose all her favourite songs. Her father, the late Elder Koledade, broke the rules of tradition by attending his own daughter's interment, as in Yorubaland or Moreso in Yagbaland, parents are not allowed to attend the burial of their children. There is a saying in both of these traditions that it is ideal for your children to bury you but not ideal for you to bury them, meaning it is frowned on if you outlive your offspring. For myself I couldn't face Bosede's funeral, as I was too upset. I had the backing of Bosede's mother, who was very worried about me. She sent a message to my parents, saying that she didn't expect me to attend.

It was a very difficult time for me, my mother and my father. I became ill and very fearful. My parents performed some African traditional rites for me, and also made sacrifices that involved the cooking of a special meal each day. They made a concession to drink, and offered charity by giving money to certain people in our society. Quoting my parents, this was supposed to 'prevent' me from 'following Bosede Koledade', meaning that I myself could die soon because of the close friendship we had. This didn't imply suicide. It was one of those beliefs. This had been my first experience of the death of a friend. I was eleven, while Bosede had been thirteen.

In Egbe I went through hell and back with Debo whenever

we were left alone at home. We argued as brothers and sisters do. He would hit me then drag me through the open path behind our backyard, along the stony ground. It hurt so much, but I never cried – I only shouted as he dragged me along. Our neighbours, Mama and Baba Folake, would shout at him, telling him to leave his sister alone. But my brother wasn't satisfied until he had dragged me to the nearest shop, called Papa Alawon's (one of our relatives), where he finally stopped. This happened many times and I suppose my body just got used to it after a while.

In 1969 I sat my common entrance exams for admission to secondary education. I failed, and so I had to sit for individual schools' exams. I took quite a few, and I finally passed one of them. I was not a very academically brilliant child, also not a very happy one either, so most of the time I did not concentrate on my class work. Yet I was very excited at the idea of going to secondary school, just like every child where we lived. I was particularly stimulated at the thought of all the new things I would be buying to take with me, and at the independence I would have.

Chapter Five

In 1970 the civil war ended. Major-General Yakubu Gowon led the Nigerian armed forces and the government to a settlement. With the war over, everything was more relaxed and peaceful. I was in secondary school, Form One. By this time, I had had lots of young boys who wanted to be my pen pals, as they were referred to in those days, not boyfriends. My father would not have allowed any hint of the latter at such a young age, though I doubt he'd know about it anyway – which was not the case with my mother. He was known throughout the town as very strict, a man who would stop paying my school fees if he knew I had a boyfriend. For this reason I settled for a pen pal, or rather several, as a great many letters were written to me from boys in neighbouring schools. Some of my friends had the same experience. We would go through our letters in our spare time, and we replied to every single one. Some even included their photographs, but my answer to their requests to be my boyfriend was always no: my heart was set on this one particular boy I had met during the holidays. His name was Adesola Daniyan, who became my boyfriend for seven years, which initially was kept a secret.

I had become a young woman. Adesola was in Form Five, but his school was very far away from mine, in a different town and state. I received his letters twice a week, and I replied in kind. It was very romantic, and we were very much in love. We made sure we saw each other every holiday, though meanwhile I still had boys from the other secondary schools in town trying their best to go out with me. Some, who would not take no for an answer, would sneak to see me in front of my house on their outing day. Some came with presents, poems, even letters.

I was in Egbe Girls' College, while my father had taken another appointment in Jos (Plateau State), in the northern part of Nigeria. This was before his retirement five years later. My brother, my sisters and I spent half of our holidays with him and his wife in Jos, where he took us to all the town's major attractions. I remember mostly the zoo, where we went after church and after our Sunday lunch. My father loved animals so much that he had made friends with the chief zoo keeper. We also went for long drives in our car to the neighbouring town of Bukuru, or we visited my father's friends and relatives. Sometimes we worked on his building site in an area in Jos called Jenta, where he was putting up a new house. We tended to help out here on a Sunday afternoon, a strange thing to do for churchgoers, which only points up how radical my father could sometimes be. We'd have to be on our guard and ready to play, so that none of our friends would glimpse us doing the ungodly thing.

On one of our travels from Jos to Lokoja, my father could not drive us back because of his heavy workload. Normally he would have driven us, or put us on the train, or even sent us by helicopter, a service just having started between Jos and a small aerodrome village called Odo-Eri. None of these options was available, and in any case none would have taken us directly to Lokoja Town. Instead we travelled by lorry, which took us two days. We arrived at Shintaku, five miles from Lokoja, late at night, and from here had to take a ferry where the two major rivers in Nigeria, the Niger and the Benue, meet. The next crossing was the following day, so we were obliged to sleep in the lorry, together with the driver, who was seventy, and most of the other passengers. The lorry driver counted everyone, and made sure all were deeply asleep before he crept to where I was lying. He lay down very close to me, and pressed closer and closer still. I could feel his body next to mine, and I could feel him touching my bottom. I started up and screamed very loudly, and realised that in my sleep he'd abused me. My brother Debo heard my screams and knew what had happened. He dealt severely with the lorry driver, hitting him so hard he gave him a black eye. The driver pleaded and said how sorry he was, adding he couldn't think what had come over him.

I was very proud of Adebowale. All the other passengers rebelled against the driver and refused to travel with him. On the next morning, Debo, Tokunbo and I paid extra money for the ferry to Lokoja. We narrated our tale to my mother when we got home, and her reaction was cold as usual, but she did ask if the lorry driver had actually raped me. She was thinking of possible medical treatment. I said I hadn't been raped, only molested – but what a life I had had so far, I thought to myself. Why me, a mere thirteen-year-old?

My grandmother, my sister, my brother and I lived in my father's house in Egbe, as my mother had taken an appointment in Lokoja too. I was a young woman of secondary-school status, on my own but with the supervision of my grandmother.

I shared the holidays with both parents, which was the nicest part of it. I was beginning to forget about my unhappy childhood and was enjoying the company of my new friends and my newfound freedom. I looked forward to travelling to Lokoja in the school holidays because of my boyfriend, Adesola. He spent that time with his parents out at Lokoja too. We saw each other every day during the holidays. We went to the movies once or twice a week. When he came to the house while my mother was at work, we played and listened to the latest music, like the Beatles and soul music, and danced – we were very good together. My little sister Titilola was always at home with us, and had to be bribed with twenty pence per day in order that she didn't tell my mother what was going on.

In any case, my mother was very much interested in younger men, and certainly had many of them. She had a relationship with a particular man whose nickname, so far as we were concerned, was Brother Peter. That, illogically, was because he lived with his little brother, called Peter. Brother Peter was the same age as my mother's first child, Adebowale. He lived about fifty yards away from us, and every night, or almost every night, while we were asleep in the other room, he would sneak into the living room where he and my mother had sex all night. Oblivious of what was going on the first time, I caught them in the act when I woke in the night and went for a drink from the fridge. From then on I looked out for them after midnight and always peeped at what was going on. I told my sister Tokunbo about my findings. She was very upset about it, and wouldn't ever spy with me whenever Brother Peter was having sex with our mother.

There was another boyfriend of hers, a liaison she kept in parallel with Brother Peter. This was Mr Job Omolola. It was easy for her to keep these two because Mr Omolola lived and worked in a different town and only came to stay at weekends. Growing teenagers as we were, my sister and I had to face up to all this and had no choice but to live with it. Mr Omolola was about ten to twelve years my mother's junior, just another toy boy. He was my least favourite of all her ventures, because he made me wash his underwear – singlets and pants and suchlike – and ordered me around. I would be commanded to cook, even when I could barely do so.

We were not allowed to mention any of this to my father. When she finished her relationships with these two after a few years or so, she immediately started with another man. He was called Mr Ikubolaje. She took Mr Ikubolaje more seriously, and seemed more faithful to him than with the others – except for two or three occasions around her fortieth birthday, when she went as an escort to my boyfriend's uncle, Chief Babalola Ariyo. This was to an exclusive location, a trip that lasted three days. On other occasions she went as an escort to one of our family friends, a top government official who became a prominent politician. I shall not mention his name, as it's likely to be a shock to many people.

We thought my mother loved Mr Ikubolaje – or at any rate I, personally, thought she did. For that reason I was happy for her, so I showed him a bit of friendliness, and was civil to him. Because their relationship lasted for a very long time, until he died just a few years ago, I asked my mother why she felt the need for all this escort business.

49

Her explanation was that she married my father when she was seventeen, and so did not have the privilege of exploring other men. As my mother put it, while I had the opportunity today to pick and choose whoever I wanted, she was making up for lost time. That might be fair comment, but – and call me sexist if you like – in my community, or generally in most cultures in Nigeria, or even maybe in Africa, if a man has many affairs or acquires many women, a wife is supposed to be calm and gentle and remain loyal and faithful to some extent. To me it all lacked discretion, and I always said to myself that when I grew up I would not wish to be like my mother. I always said that I would be a very good mother to my children. I am very pleased and satisfied within myself that I have managed in the situations I've found myself in, and have shown good examples and good basic principles to my children. Most of my friends do not understand and find it incredible how much I have had to endure. I am sure they will now understand why. I detested the way my mother was, flaunting all her relationships, while never at any moment thinking what effect it would have on her children.

In secondary school, we studied all the usual subjects, and for the first time in my life I was doing very well. I particularly liked French, English (literature and language), and geography and history. My school formed a debating society, which I participated in. We went into other schools to take part in their debates. Usually the topic was chosen for us, with a 'for' or 'against' the motion. I found it exhilarating because most of the time our school won. We practised lots of sports too, and I became very athletic. I did the 100 metres, long jump, relay and netball. With all of it going so well, I was beginning to think there was a meaning to life.

I spent two years at my new school, but then my parents wanted me to change. They looked for transfers in the various towns where they lived, but they were not successful. Their reasoning for such a move was that they wanted a school with a better record in its O-level results. My father took me to St Louis Girls' Secondary School in Jos, but we just missed the last vacancy by a few minutes. I liked St Louis, but I would have to have been a boarder if I'd got in, because I would have loathed to live with my father and his second wife at that time. Eventually, I found a school in Mopa in Kogi State – my mother's town. My grandparents, great-grandmother, great-aunts and great-uncles still lived there, so it was not too bad for me at all. It was a mixed school, which of course was not the case with my last. I started at Mopa ECWA Secondary School in my third year. I soon made new friends but I was not quite as happy as in Egbe Girls' School.

In 1972 Nigeria had the National Festival of Arts. All schools in Nigeria participated, as did professional actors and comedians. Mopa Secondary took part in drama and dance, representing Kwara State, of which Mopa formed a part before the recent creation of further states, which merged Mopa into Kogi State. The festival took place in Kaduna in the Northern State of Nigeria. On our journey there, my school and all the participants stayed at the Queen Elizabeth Secondary School in Ilorin, Kwara State, for one week's rehearsals with the rest of our state participants. It was fun and I felt a sense of privilege. I took part in drama, and I was the leading actor, playing the part of a boy (and so I was dressed as a man). We had rehearsals every day and we watched other people perform as well. There was dancing, with acrobatic dancers, and all that sort of thing. There were also other drama groups from a range of different schools. After our rehearsals we all stayed at the All Festival of Arts Village in Kaduna, a community built especially for the occasion. My school enacted a play called *Agbalowomeri*. It won us third position – third in the whole country – with me a leading actor! I was so proud. The government paid us a lot of pocket money while at the village, and we were there for three weeks. Then all the contestants travelled back to their various states, at which point disaster struck. The coach in which the Western State group were travelling crashed and several contestants were killed. A prominent and well-known Nigerian playwright and actor from the University of Ibadan – Mr Duro Ladipo – was also killed. The Kwara State coaches were, fortunately, far behind them, and we were lucky not to be affected. It was all so sad.

Back in Mopa, my grandmother and all her friends had been listening to the transistor radio every hour to hear the latest news and to know that we were safe. We were welcomed home as heroes, and my school was proud of us all.

I wanted to become a journalist on leaving secondary school, and so my mother took me to the Nigerian Television Authority (NTA) in Kaduna. There I was shown round the newsroom and studio. My escort explained how the news was edited before being read by a newscaster. He sat me down at the news desk and told me to pretend to read the hourly news. I noticed you could see yourself on screen while in that process, which I imagined could be slightly unnerving. In the end, however, I was unable to get into journalism because I didn't pass the required papers, and therefore there was no form of scholarship available.

I continued in Mopa Secondary with lots of sports. I played centre in our netball team. To that I added basketball and volleyball. I did the long jump, ran the 100 metres, and I always came first in the inter-schools' competitions. I was also a winner in the 440-metres relay. On the social side, the Mopa Student Union organised a lot of discos for the students, either at weekends or during the Christmas holidays. There were big dancing competitions, attracting teenagers with their parents, and students from neighbouring towns and even from Lagos. In December 1972 a competition was held at the Oba of Mopa's palace (the late Oba Orimolade;an oba is a traditional ruler of a community or leader of various communities or local authorities). It involved all the other schools in the area and students from abroad. I came second, and I can still remember the white and pink hotpants I wore, bought for me by my father. Everyone admired the get-up, including the old grandmothers who had come to watch. My own grandmother was very proud, but my parents weren't exactly over the moon. I find it quite striking nowadays that my daughter is so much like me in some of the things she does in school – dance and drama to a very high standard – though I see she has much of her dad in her too.

Students and teenagers, ranging from thirteen to sixteen years old, came to Mopa with their parents or guardians looking for love, mostly during the Christmas holidays. Here we all looked out for prospective husbands, with arranged marriages very much part of the culture. You could see these negotiations going on among the parents, where it was important to learn of the job prospects of any potential candidate, what the family background was, proneness to sickness or disease, temperament, and family background generally. Looks came into it too. Once all these things had been weighed and considered, the parents on both sides became almost as one. I would say that about ninety-five per cent of all such arrangements produced happy, successful relationships. For myself, I had already got a boyfriend, but it was a relationship that lasted for seven years before Adesola and I went our separate ways.

I took my O levels in 1974. I did not pass, so I had to retake the following year, when I did a little better – enough to get me through life. However, towards the end of Year Five, the whole class held a demonstration, believe it or not. I cannot remember what this was about, but some from Year Five beat up the younger students after prep class in the evening. It was a very big issue with the school authority and the headteacher. He called out names in assembly the following morning, and for one reason or another mine kept recurring. That astonished me, as I hadn't beaten anyone up, though I had shouted a lot and protested. The headteacher did not believe my plea. All but about ten from our class were suspended for a period of six months, which took us into the next O-level sitting.

My mother looked for a temporary school for me, so that I could use their laboratory and join in the science experiments. My own school allowed those who were suspended back in to sit their exams, which was a traumatic time for all of us, especially me. We were called names, and we were looked upon in the village as local thugs and troublemakers. Nevertheless, once we'd taken our exams we had our graduation ceremony, which my parents attended. I chose the hymns 'Guide Me O Thou Great Jehovah' and 'Gracious Things of Thee are Spoken – Zion, City of our God' for my graduation ceremony.

My father had been to Oxford University in England, in 1955–56, a year before I was born. He read English. He also had the privilege of meeting Her Majesty the Queen, personally, in 1955, being among the Nigerian Oxford student delegation sent to Buckingham Palace. He was enormously proud of this, and grateful for it for the rest of his life. We still have the photographs hanging on our living-room wall, showing his handshake with Her Majesty. He told us so much about England, almost every day. Because it had been one of his own better times, he was full of nostalgia for the experience. It inspired me, and because he wanted his children to study in England, it was always on my mind to travel there. When I discussed this with my family, my father, mother and uncle didn't object.

Now that my father had retired, money was tight. We had to manage with what we'd got, and this meant he was unable to pay my tuition fees and the expense of travelling to England. I had to work and save before I could go. I travelled from Lokoja to Lagos, the capital of Nigeria, in order to retake my papers and go to college and look for a job. I lived with my mother's uncle and his family, the late Chief Ade-John (he died in 1998). I was there for three years. While in Lagos, I worked as a kindergarten teacher at a school owned by Mrs Ade-John. She paid me £17.50 a month. I taught children from the age of three to five, but this was only a temporary job. As I was not a trained teacher there were no long-term prospects for me here. I then worked for a company for six months, and went to evening class to retake further O levels, which would get me to college. I was earning good money, but I didn't get carried away with it.

In 1975 I read in one of the state newspapers that my mother had changed her name and no longer wished to bear my father's name. Where she had been Mrs Martha Abiodun she was now Miss Nathaniel Aborisade. She also wanted to start divorce proceedings against my father, which I strongly opposed. In the 1970s in Nigeria this was a very unusual thing to do, almost regarded as not respectable. Divorce proceedings were more commonly filed by men. Women tended to stay in an unhappy relationship – first because of the children, and second for financial reasons, men usually being the breadwinners. Where there was domestic violence, and even when men had extra-marital affairs, women still stayed, having very little power to do otherwise.

I had a telegram from my mother telling me of her intentions. I worked hard to stop the divorce, naïvely perhaps. Had I known then what I know now about relationships and marriage, I would not have stood in her way. I supposed she had her own reasons for doing what she did, but nevertheless I travelled all the way to Ilorin, to Pategi, to Bacita – in fact, anywhere I had to in order to reason with the various members of her family. All this I did over a period of three to four days, travelling by luxury bus, a service out of Lagos called Ekeleodilichukwu. On that bus, I cried pretty much all of the time. I did, however, persuade her family to call a meeting, and for the sake of us, her children, I succeeded in calling a halt to the divorce. This was quite an achievement, since in Nigerian society if you weren't married you were regarded as a lesser and unimportant

My father in 1955 with Her Majesty the Queen at Buckingham Palace.

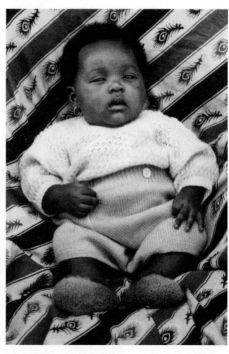

father Micah Abiodun.

Me at 2½ months old.

Me in England.

Me in England.

My Father, Mother and sister Toks.

My Father in college.

yself at the age of 15 years old.

My Father on the left, my grandfather on the right.

and my Grandmother.

Me at my flat in Ilorin, Nigeria.

Me at a dinner organise
in London.

My son Joseph.

My son Joseph and daughter Rebecca.

person. Furthermore, when things went wrong it was always the women who were blamed. If there is one thing I have learnt from other people's cultural attitudes towards marriage, it is simply that you should not stay in a relationship for the sake of the children. The effects this has over time are not worth it, especially for the children themselves. Could I advise my mother now, I would advise differently. I single-handedly got my parents back together again, which is how they remained married until my father died – married, though living in different houses (with my father's other wife still with him). It was something my brothers and sisters thanked me for, not to mention my mother's family. And it was a huge issue at the time, the children of divorced women having hardly any rights, and regarded as second-class citizens. I think differently now, because I believe that compatibility and love are very important in any relationship, and perhaps regret that my mother had to reverse her claim in the regional papers regarding her change of name.

Chapter Six

My uncle and aunt, Chief and Mrs Ade-John, went on a three-week summer holiday to London. I stayed at home with all the children and the domestic staff. My two cousins had a big party in our large living room. Myself, most of their family friends and a lot of teenagers were invited. It was a great party. When it ended, and all the guests had gone, and almost everyone at home had gone to bed, I was called downstairs to do some chores with other members of my family. I was raped by my two cousins, one after the other, and was powerless to resist. I was seventeen and a half. I have kept this secret with me for a very long time, and have decided not to mention the two men's names here in my book (though my children know who they were). At that time in Nigeria, society saw to it that the victims of rape were ashamed to report it or complain to the police, the attitude being that the woman was always complicit in the crime. 'She asked for it.' One was also made to feel intimidated, and treated like a leper. For that reason ninety-nine per cent of rape cases went unreported. It was outrageous for me to see these people who'd committed such awful acts going about their businesses as if nothing at all had happened, and they were innocent men. Often such people had very high office and were seen as pillars of our country. It was galling too, that if I bumped into them, once in five years or so at some family function, we all knew each other's secrets. I detested them so much! This whole issue has affected me in so many ways throughout my life, and I find it very painful to talk about.

I gained admission to the Federal Training Centre in Lagos, which was a college for typists. I soon got my twenty-five words per minute, and I was able to get a better paid job. I was posted to Lagos's Federal Ministry of Works, where I worked as a typist for six months. One other good thing that happened there was that I met my best friend, Belinda Okonweze. We went to various clubs and house parties with some of our other friends. Two clubs I remember were the Octopus at Akerele in Surulere, and the Beachcomber at Ikeja, both in Lagos. We also went to the Super Cinema near Shitta-Bay in Surulere, where we watched *Bisi, Daughter of the River*, a film that featured Patti Boulaye in the main role.

The following year I took another examination at another Federal Training Centre, which took me to my next typing stage and into shorthand. This was at Ilorin, Kwara State, and so I moved out of Lagos, for eighteen months, during 1976–77. We students lived in a hostel, where we cooked for ourselves, the Federal Government of Nigeria paying us a monthly allowance. This was called 'in-service training'. It was a fun time, very wild, my best time to date, as I think was the case for many of my friends. We partied at weekends and met a great many men, to the point that I changed my boyfriend as often as I changed my clothes (I had finished with Adesola, so perhaps I did this to console the loss). We had money to spend and were well fed, and were up with the latest fashions. Friends I made at this time were Bolanle Adeyemi, Kosor Chukurah, Irene Adjudua, Mrs Ogbogu, Mosunmola Ogunlana, Tolani Akinrinade, Dolapo Ebizua and the late Jumoke Ogundalu.

Once I went out with a man who collected my friends and me in a helicopter. We would be picked up from Ilorin Airport at a given time, and from there travel to Lagos or Benin City. The man in question was an Air Vice-Marshal in the Nigerian Air Force, about eighteen or twenty years older than me. Because he was married he wanted me to keep the affair secret. It was very hard for me to do that, but except for a few friends knowing, and my aunt, I did manage to keep it under wraps. He travelled alone whenever we went anywhere, usually to exclusive guesthouses. He gave me expensive gifts, which I found enticing. Whenever a bunch of us got to Benin City on one of these weekend breaks, it was always the intention of the men to have sex with us. I, however, always played my little tricks, with flimsy complaints, because believe it or not I was only interested in the gifts, travelling on the helicopter and meeting interesting people, especially influential dignitaries. I would pretend to be unwell, or said I needed more time, and silly things like that. It worked most of the time, but of course there were occasions when it didn't, and so I had to have sex. When we didn't have sex the Air Vice-Marshal tended to get annoyed and upset, but because he was very caring his anger only lasted a short time, and we always made up.

So, at the age of nineteen or twenty, everything was so much fun. It was a form of security, all the pampering I got, and the knowledge that someone cared for me, after all the lack of love I had experienced in my early life. When I came to England a year or two later, to further my education, he asked one of his officers in the Air Force, who was designated to London, to phone me from time to time, and to help me financially if that was what was needed. I didn't ever take advantage of this opportunity, preferring to work hard on my own once I got to England. But he was very good to me whenever he himself travelled here, arriving with lots of interesting gifts, which sometimes were foodstuffs, the delicacies he thought I might have missed. He wanted me to know how much he cared for me, and told me many times how proud of me he was, because of my independence. I found this so very encouraging, and I determined not to let him down. I studied harder and worked to make ends meet, and all the while he treated me with so much kindness, which was unusual in an affair of this type. My friends were amazed at his attitude, because common to their relationships was an awareness of being treated as tools for sex. It remained an on–off liaison until I met my present husband, who, when I fell in love with him, made me begin to think that I should stop these adventures with other men. This is really what told me I was in love, and so from then on all other relationships ceased.

My mother worked and lived at Ilorin, while my father stayed in Egbe, with his other wife. On my side I saved enough money while at the training centre to buy my ticket for England, and left Ilorin in 1977, with thirty-five words per minute typing. This was an improvement, but I would still need to achieve 50 words per minute, and 120 in shorthand – otherwise I couldn't earn the good money a top secretary could expect. I was still planning ahead for Pitman's Central College in England.

I worked for a year after I had been posted back from

Ilorin to Lagos, at the Police Affairs Department, in Victoria Island, where I was tempted to give up on my England dream. I had made new friends in high society, and I mixed with my boss's friends, and also went out with Mr Francis Okeke himself. He was a permanent secretary, while my direct manager was a personal assistant, Mrs Elizabeth Kemi-Shadare. I went to parties and official functions with them, and was given the job of secretarial typist to the permanent secretary. All my friends from before were posted to Lagos too, so we tried to see each other often.

I did not like the Lagos life, and never have. There was corruption everywhere, and for a young girl like myself it was not the best place to live. My parents were not too keen either. But I worked hard for my future, and in 1978 I had saved almost as much as I needed. I begged my mother to help towards the remaining amount, which she did. She gave me half of my school fees, and my late uncle, Chief Ade-John, gave me money too. In 1979 I had amassed £1,500. This was for a year's tuition at Pitman's, though I later spent two years there, having accumulated £5,000. Accommodation and transport costs had to be thought about too.

By the end of 1978 I had applied to Pitman's and was lucky enough to get an admission for 1979. There were lots of arrangements to be made, with much paperwork concerning my visa that had to be directed through the Cabinet Office and the British High Commission. It was all very demanding, and to add to it all I needed to nominate a guarantor, who happened to be Chief Ade-John. Eventually we managed to get everything in order, with Mr Okeke and Elizabeth Shadare helping with the Cabinet Office part. Then came forms for yellow fever, a vaccine for which was administered by my sister Tokunbo's husband, Dr Segun Mathew. But at last I got my one-year visa, and so was fully equipped for my journey to England.

As my departure date drew nearer, I travelled frequently to Egbe, Mopa and Ilorin, to see my father, mother and grandmother. It was hectic. I finally travelled to England on 8 August 1979, on an evening flight, with British Caledonian Airways. My friends and my cousin's wife saw me off at the Murtala Muhammed Airport, Lagos. I arrived at Heathrow at about 6 a.m. I remember I felt very cold, despite the fact that it wasn't even winter. Before passing through Immigration and Customs I was put in the medical room, for an X-ray, which passed me fit. The X-ray operator explained that because I was a student, and not a visitor, this was normal procedure. Immigration went well, but in Customs I was so nervous that, despite having nothing to declare, I considered myself lucky not to be stopped. I had heard many tales of the things that happened in airports.

I got out with my luggage trolley and waited for my cousin, Stephen Aiyelayin. I was going to be staying with him, and we were supposed to be meeting at the airport, but we missed each other. I took a black cab to his house in Leyton, east London. I gave the driver the address, and he knew it immediately and took me there. It was a long way from the airport – it took such a long time, and I was charged £15. As we drove along I remained fixated looking out of the window, taking in the views of London. It all looked huge compared with Lagos, and my first impression was that it was neater too.

It was a cold but sunny August day, and Stephen arrived

some time later from the airport, having failed to find me. His landlord and landlady were Mr and Mrs Oladiti. I called them Uncle and Aunty even though I wasn't related. They were both very nice to me throughout my two-and-a-half-year stay.

I spent my first week in England going out every day. Stephen showed me everywhere. First we went to the shops, then to Dalston market, and we followed that with the supermarkets. He showed me how to take the buses and Underground, which I learnt very quickly and got on with very well. Towards the end of the week he took me to Pitman's in Southampton Row, WC1. We checked on the deposit I had paid, and having gone to the bank to open an account I also paid the balance on my fees. I had about a month before starting college, and so had very little time to be homesick. I shopped for my winter clothes, any books I needed, and for stationery and food.

I soon had to change many of the things I did, or the way I did them, and also adapt to my new way of life. I didn't mind this, and didn't see it as a problem. One of the changes was cooking, where I often had to find alternative ingredients, since there wasn't quite the global availability then as now. I also had to adapt to the cold weather, though I loved it when it snowed, and soon learned to wrap up warm. I had to be careful with money, and not spend too much unnecessarily. Most of all I had to work extremely hard, both at my studies and at the weekend jobs I found. And I had to get used to not having a boyfriend around.

I did cleaning jobs after school and I worked at a bingo hall, which gave me extra money. This took up my time from 5 a.m. to 10.30 p.m., but I was full of energy and coped with it well. The bingo hall was just around the corner from where I lived, and I would get back home at about 11 p.m. I'd have a bath and a snack, and then did my homework if I had any. Anyone who knows about shorthand can tell you you need to drill at least half an hour or an hour every day, in order to acquire a good speed. I did about half an hour every night before I went to bed, by which time it was usually 12.30 a.m.

College was very hard work, but for me it was toil laced with pleasure. I enjoyed being at Pitman's – it was all a new experience for me. I met people from all walks of life, and from other countries. I made friends with people from all over the world, such as Grace Kissi and Julie Anno-Okanta from Ghana, Maja from Iran, Bijal from Tanzania, Nike and Mabel from Nigeria, and others from Kuwait, China and Japan. Grace and Bijal still live in London, so I see them regularly. Julie is in America, while many others went back to live in their various home countries. We also had a few older students in some of our classes, secretaries or permanent assistants sent from the Houses of Parliament to brush up on their general secretarial skills. There were always parties and clubs to go to every weekend, Friday to Sunday. We worked hard but we had a social life too.

I met one of my boyfriends, called Dave, on the tube, one busy morning going to college. He followed me and invited me for a drink after work, which I accepted. He was very polite, which was one of the first things that struck me about him. We went out a couple of times, and before we knew it we started seeing each other seriously. All my friends in college met him. He visited me a lot at my house in Leyton too, and each time we saw each other we made love. Our affair lasted for over three months. I thought he was so sweet and polite, until one of my friends, Julie, who used to live in his street, discovered somehow that he was separated from his wife. I did not believe it at first, because for one reason she didn't like the idea of my going out with a white person. She made it clear when she met Dave that she didn't like him. However, as Dave didn't tell me about this separation, or indeed much about himself, I did suspect that he was hiding things from me, and so that was the end of the relationship. The next time he phoned me I told him so. He pleaded with me, saying how sorry he was, but I put an end to it. I did like him though.

I worked, I had money in the bank, and my mother sent me £100 in bank drafts from time to time. I indulged in designer wear and I lived above my budget. I shopped at Marks and Spencer, Selfridges, Top Shop, Wallis and Jane Norman – in fact, almost all the high street stores, so every penny counted.

I often saw my cousins, uncles and aunts here in England on business trips or attending training courses. My favourite cousin was captain of a ship, the *River Jimini*. He is called Captain Omotesho. He would organise parties on his ship, which I went to with friends. I sometimes sailed on his ship, from Tilbury to Middlesbrough or Middlesbrough to Liverpool. Then, opportunely, all these visiting relatives of mine would ask me to help them with something or other, cooking or shopping, or simply allowing them to meet my friends – all of which would be enough for them to give me £200, sometimes £500. This extra money helped me to keep going, which was very welcome when, after a year's tuition at Pitman's, I spent another year getting a diploma.

That meant another year's school fees, so you can see, anything I could get was gratefully received. That said, money from Nigeria was slow, and it was always difficult for my mother.

I rented a bedroom in the house I shared with my cousin Stephen. One of my uncles, Mr Adebisi Martin – who was a successful businessman – owned a fifteen-bedroom place in Gerrards Cross, Buckinghamshire. He got in touch with me in 1981, wanting a housekeeper – not a job I could take on, as it would be too much to combine with my college work. I offered to shop and cook for him and his guests and business partners whenever they were visiting, and this he took me up on. He gave me a room in his house and paid me £1,000 a month. I was thrilled, and did the job to the best of my ability. It meant I could give up my other odd jobs, which left me juggling between Gerrards Cross and London. I spent most of my weekends in Buckinghamshire, where it was all so beautiful and peaceful. My friends Grace and Julie came to see me at weekends.

The house was always full of visitors from Italy, America and Nigeria, and very busy. I was virtually responsible for the people who stayed there, ensuring there was enough food and that the cooking went to plan. Mr Adebisi Martin later employed proper housekeepers – a Mr and Mrs Taylor from Manchester. They did a good job, especially with the gardening. I re-visited the house some few years ago, before it was sold for £1.5 million. My friends and I had a good time there and I thought things could not have been better for me in view of the pay.

I had met a man called Ademola Ibiyeye when getting ready to travel to England from Nigeria. He had come to

Nigeria on holiday from Canada, because his mother had died. We exchanged addresses and we chatted a lot before he returned across the Atlantic. When I was in England he wrote to me regularly – in fact, the very first letter arrived before I did! I went on holiday to Canada to visit him – Fredericton, New Brunswick – for a three-week stay. We had a wonderful time, and we fell in love. He proposed, and we were engaged, so now I overstayed my holiday by a week. All my friends phoned me to say I was in trouble with my classes. But never mind: I met all Ademola's friends, at discos and parties. We were invited out for dinner, and we toured many of the other towns around New Brunswick. Finally I returned to London. Demola sent me an engagement ring by post, guessing the size of my finger, and luckily it fitted. He came to visit me in the September of 1980. I was twenty-two and he was twenty-five. We got married and were to live in Nigeria after he had finished his university education in Canada. However, we did not live together for more than two weeks after the marriage, and the marriage was annulled.

My father was diagnosed with diabetes. He was getting old and his health had deteriorated. I went back for the Christmas of 1980 to see him, returning to London in January 1981. He died on 4 February at the age of sixty-eight, just a month after I'd left him. I was devastated, even though I'd seen it coming. Sadly, I was unable to attend the funeral service, with my major exams coming up. I travelled back to Nigeria afterwards, in April 1981, to visit his grave and to see my mother and all the family and friends who had helped.

I sat my exams in early April 1981, passing my thirty-five words per minute in typing, and eighty in shorthand. We were allowed to take our exams once every month, if we were ready. I decided to take my next one in June/July, and I passed my 50 words per minute in typing and 100 in shorthand. I was so pleased with myself. Then I passed my other subjects too, getting my Advanced Diploma in Secretarial Studies.

Chapter Seven

I went back to Nigeria in January 1982, having bought many household things to take with me, and shipping everything via my cousin's boat, the *River Jimini*. I didn't waste time looking for a job, and in Ilorin, I was made two offers – one was with the state government and the other at the University of Ilorin. I accepted the university offer, because it paid better, and came with housing benefits and transport facilities. I was confidential secretary to the dean of one of the faculties.

I settled down and looked for a flat, and my belongings arrived a few weeks later. My dear friend Ms Dolapo Ajagbona, a solicitor, helped me find a flat. I stayed with another friend of mine, Tessy Agboli, for the two months before the place was ready. It was brand new, and I was the first to move in. The university paid half the rent, and the transportation they provided took me to work and back. My job was a highly responsible one – I had a whole team of typists, with office clerks and messengers also managed by me. I worked long hours, my boss regularly keeping me behind for long shorthand dictations.

Dolapo moved in to the flat adjacent to mine, and we saw each other every day – so I certainly wasn't lonely. I organised parties every two weeks, and I sometimes went to get-togethers, preparing much of the food myself. I also did a lot of travelling, using my three weeks' annual leave as well as sick leave. I usually went to London, where I saw my friends and stayed with Grace Kissi. Once there I did a little business to supplement my day job, such as the purchase of shoes and bags at London's wholesale stores, to sell them on for a higher price in Nigeria. I made three trips a year, able to pay for them from the profits I made. My buyers in Ilorin were shopkeepers.

On one of our London trips, Dolapo and I stayed at one of the bed-and-breakfast hotels. She had come to shop for her wedding (a wedding, as it turned out, that was never to be). We overstayed when Lagos Airport was closed, there having been another coup d'état in Nigeria. Needless to say, we left London as soon as the airport was re-opened.

In 1983 my itinerary was Lagos–Rome–London–Rome–Lagos. In Rome I had some business, buying shoes and bags for re-sale, for which there was now great demand in Nigeria. I socialised too, meeting up with some Nigerian students who drove me to Florence. I stayed the night with one of them. Later I took the train from Rome to Naples.

Three months after I moved to my flat my grandmother came to stay with me. She was exceedingly helpful, and this I will always cherish. She cooked breakfast, lunch and dinner – not only for me but for my friends and for Dolapo too. She also cleaned the house and did the gardening, and, generally, was great company. She remained with me until I left for London in 1984.

I met one of my best friends in 1982 in the Department of Business Studies, while I was waiting to be allocated to a boss. His name was Dr Paul Zarboski. He was a geologist, and we first met when he came to photocopy a document in my office. We did not see each other again until a couple of months later, when I was posted to the Department of Biochemistry in another campus entirely. His department shared a building with ours, so we saw each other every day. When we started going out he would give me a lift home from work and then pick me up from my flat and take me to his. We went shopping together sometimes, and at other times booked our holiday flights on the same plane. We would meet in London and socialise there. I have to say that although we did a lot of things together, I was not in love with him, and for that reason the relationship went nowhere. We did, however, like each other a lot, so we decided to remain friends. More recently he spent time in London (about three years), but returned to Zaria, Nigeria, in 2000, to take up a new appointment at the Ahmadu Bello University. He had been a lecturer in Nigeria for many years.

My sister Tokunbo got married in December 1982, which was a big family occasion. I travelled to the Republic of Benin to buy some of the things needed for the ceremony, and took a friend, Dr David Atteh, with me. We had to smuggle clothing and alcohol back into Nigeria, but we did so without getting caught. Two weeks after the wedding my great-grandmother, Ma Ruth Aiyelayin, died, so there were two rites of passage that year in our family.

When my great-grandmother was alive, the kitchen was the richest part of the house – richer even than the backyard, with its many pigs, and goats, and snakes, and its guava, cashew and orange trees. It's a vivid memory because in the kitchen, cooking was delegated on a per-person basis, depending on who was eating the same type of meal.

There was, for example, a quota for teenagers, and another for younger children, in which category I happened to be. Being a very large household, each cooking regime was directed by the most senior wives. I watched and helped as the meals were prepared. Responsibilities included pounding yam in the mortar and preparing soup, stews and meals for the younger ones.

My great-grandmother had a special way of eating her food. With her pounded yam, she would mould it round like dough and ditch it in the middle of her palm, adding the soup or stew or sometimes both, while eating her meat separately. This was because she had lost all her teeth. She shared her food with us, as we knelt down to greet her after our long journey, travelling by road from the town or city. She made us stretch out our hands, right or left, depending on which you used, serving into our open palms. My friends – Dapo Abanida and Kehinde Alaya, and another friend – all experienced this. They laughed so heartily that I laughed too, unable to help myself. So did Ma Ruth. It was in this way that my great-grandmother shared her food with many of the guests who came to see her. She was generous and unique, and full of special qualities.

The last time I had this type of meal with her was at the spinsters' night organised by my mother's family, with other extended families and friends. It was for my sister, Tokunbo, and her husband, Segun. The event took place at Ile Loke, the main house Ma Ruth shared with her late husband, Pa Joshua Aiyelayin, where she had always lived. She was too old to walk down the big stairs of the house, but she was not too old to eat her special ogun soup or okoro and meat soup (ila asepo). Ogun soup was plugged from one of the plants that grew in the backyard of the house in the compound. It was dark red before it was made into soup, and dark red when thoroughly cooked. It was very tasty – delicious, in fact – and was eaten with pounded yam (yam boiled, cooked, then pounded in a mortar), or with okoro and meat soup. Okoro and meat soup is okra cooked with various ingredients together with meat and palm oil.

I managed to eat all these foods with her as I grew up, including the ones she enjoyed and those she could no longer eat on account of her age. When I left the village completely I would return for visits such as these – to see my grandmother, Abigeal, and sometimes my grandfather, Nathaniel Aborisade, and all the rest of the family and the few friends I had in the village.

At Ile Loke, money was exchanged. Little girls and boys of my age sold old or unwanted money, or even pretend money, in exchange for currency. We sold to the grown-ups in higher education or colleges, who were already earning because of their college status. The more persuasive we were, the more money we made. This all took place at Matilda's cenotaph.

Matilda was my great-great-grandmother, who died in 1938 when my mother was growing up. She was a very tall and dark-complexioned woman. This information was engraved on her monument, which bore a real photograph of her.

Baba Karahinre and Mama Karahinre were buskers. They were both born blind. Baba Karahinre brought many instruments with him, and played them in front of the compound. These included flute and tambourine. When they played and sang together, it was all very musical. There was a great deal of dancing, even as Mama Karahinre carried her twins on her back, with the aid of a large woven cloth called an oja. Baba Karahinre sang while his wife danced tirelessly. The words of the song were as follows:

Mama Karahinre re
Mama Karahinre re
Mama Karahinre re

Mama Karahinre danced and replied:

Baba Karahinre re
Baba Karahinre re
Baba Karahinre re
Mama Karahinre re

Their other two children joined in the chorus.

One of our senior wives, acting as head chef at Ruth Aiyelayin's kitchen, had four sets of twins, and she too carried these on her back with a woven cloth. They danced backwards and forwards together until they all met at the spot they had started from. All this was in front of the compound, where we all put money into their baskets. The older ones, including my grandmother Abigeal's younger sister, my great-aunt Lydia, would go reluctantly in search of her purse or wallet. I think she was stingy.

When my father was at the peak of his political life, on his way from campaigning or touring, he arrived with his full entourage. Ma Ruth Aiyelayin would prepare for everybody according to what they ate, be they vegetarian or meat or fish eaters (or those who ate only dried smoked fish). My father enjoyed the novelty. I sat beside Grandmother Abigeal looking left and right to see – with some trepidation – which food I would eat first. It could be one of her specialities, which was in her big shopping bag, waiting to be eaten by her mother, or I might have to eat off my father's plate, Mr Micah Michael Abiodun, her son-in-law.

Now to my great-grandfather, Pa Joshua Aiyelayin. His portrait hung on the wall, very static-looking. Each day since his death, my great-grandmother, Ma Ruth Aiyelayin, knelt down almost in greeting of her husband. Then, as she passed, she said, 'My lord and my husband,' or 'My father,' which amounted to the same thing to her.

I asked her once, 'Is that your father?'

She smiled and said, 'No, he is my lord,' and at a glance I saw her eyes full of tears, so I knew how much he meant to her.

Due to the 1983 coup I had overstayed my annual leave by a week, with the airport in Lagos closed. I was given a warning when I got back to work, and was then transferred to another campus and another new boss. The authorities thought that was punishment for me, yet at first it presented no problem at all. However, as time went on I had very little work to do, as my typist was doing everything. I was prone to be a workaholic, so I didn't like sitting around being bored. I also disagreed with a lot of things that went on in Nigeria at that time, the changes in and system of government generally. My decision was to resign. I applied for a degree course in business studies at a university in England. When my friend Paul brought me the letter telling me my application had been accepted, I was naturally very thrilled.

So, I was preparing to leave Nigeria for England again, but it was tougher this time because I had to leave behind so many things – my flat, my business, my family and friends. But I had made up my mind and I was determined to leave. I broke these plans gently to my mother and other important members of the family, then, in the January of 1984, I left to live in London for a second time. On arrival I went straight to Gerrards Cross. Mr and Mrs Taylor welcomed me with open arms, but now there was also a lady staying there, called Miss Oyelude, a friend of Adebisi Martin. She said she had been given instructions from him that no guest should be welcomed at the house. I pleaded with her to let me stay, if only until I could find alternative accommodation, but she didn't relent. I left in a matter of days and started looking for somewhere else. I went to a bed-and-breakfast hotel in Paddington, but by now my money was draining away quickly. Then I met a man who suggested it would be cheaper if I stayed at the YWCA. There was one in Great Russell Square in Tottenham Court Road, which fortunately had a vacancy. I stayed there for a few months, paying seventy-seven pounds a week. It had a cafeteria, where I could eat, and all in all it was a good, safe place to stay. I needed to move quickly, however, for somewhere to rent, and a job, otherwise I'd be stuck.

Slowly, things began to go wrong, and not as I had planned. I had lost my right to accommodation at Gerrards Cross, and I found everything difficult, and so unlike my first experience of living in England. I was spending my school fees on accommodation, and my prospect of going to university was doubtful. Adding to these complications, I had changed my original plans and now wanted to study law, not business studies. I picked up some brochures at the University of London, and looked at ways of retaking some of my A levels, as a first step towards that law degree. I was to end up in Canterbury in Kent, for a one-year spell at a college there. I paid a deposit on my fees, which was £800, the whole costing £1,500 in total. I was due to start in the April of 1984, but it was very doubtful that I could meet the fees in full, let alone the accommodation costs.

While at the YWCA I was friendly with a lady called Irene Jarman, who told me she had a room to let in her flat. At the same time there was a job going in the hostel itself. I was delighted at these two offers and jumped at them both. Irene was the YWCA receptionist, and the job she told me about was as typist for the then Director of the YWCA, Mrs Bellington. I got the job and moved in with Irene, for which I paid thirty-eight pounds a week. This gave me a room in Frognal Lane, Hampstead in north London. It was a lot of money for me to pay, my wages being seventy-five pounds a week after tax. I trimmed my budget though, and soon I was on an even keel.

Irene and I enjoyed living together. She organised parties and introduced me to her friends. We also had drinks together after work. On Saturdays, we took turns to shop, and we also shared the cooking. I was single at this time, without a boyfriend, so Irene was ready to match-make from among her friends. I met lots of single men, but I wasn't interested or attracted to any of them. Then one evening she told me she was having friends of hers to dinner, which I didn't think anything of. I didn't join them after work, going straight to my room to watch television. But after a while she called me down to meet her friend Jimmy Webster. We chatted for five minutes or so, and he invited me for a drink later in the week, a Thursday evening in fact. I met up with him and my first impression was that he had a good sense of humour. We spent the evening in a wine bar near where I lived, and when we came back to my flat I was tipsy without being drunk. He stayed the night. After that we phoned each other several times a day, and saw each other a lot. One weekend Irene went away to her parents' house, so we were alone in the flat, behaving like teenage lovers. We made love all day everywhere in the house – in the bath, on the floor – and hardly ate a thing. I felt good, but when Irene came back she was not very happy, especially with me.

It was obvious by now that I couldn't go to college to retake my A levels, and neither could I go to university. I settled into my job, and kept on trying hard to get a better paid one. I returned to Canterbury to redeem my deposit, having written and phoned several times. Then as time went on, it became clear that Irene hated the idea of Jimmy and me going out with each other. She resented the fact that I had taken her friend away from her. She had a boyfriend of her own, and once I'd discounted the idea that there was something more than friendship between her and Jimmy, I couldn't see what her problem was. After about three months we fell out, in a particularly nasty way. We had a big row and I moved out.

I had joined the gym at the YWCA, and this was where I worked out. The young lady in charge there, Tania, heard that I was moving out of Irene's flat, and as she had just bought one in South Kensington, she was looking for someone to share. I moved in for six weeks. It was a luxurious one-bedroom place, with two beds in the room we shared. It had a beautiful kitchen, though I was not allowed to cook there. Jimmy often came to see me here, but did not like the idea of my having to go to restaurants for all my meals. He invited me to stay with him and his friend James, in the house they shared in Park Royal, North London. At first I was reluctant to go, but he pointed out that as I could soon be looking for somewhere else anyway, I might as well. There seemed to be logic in his argument, so, in July 1984, I moved in with him.

We were very much in love, and I even got my breakfast in bed every day. Jimmy sang to me and made silly jokes, and I thought it all lovely. We went to parties and concerts, and I remember one summer afternoon we went to watch a Sunny Ade concert. Sunny Ade is a Nigerian musician.

I still worked at the YWCA, but by now I felt the pay wasn't so good, so I started looking for another job. I was called to a number of interviews, and was made two offers. I chose the firm my friend Belinda recommended to me, which was called Africonsult Ltd, situated in the Tottenham Court Road. They dealt mainly with the export of aeroplanes to Tanzania and Kenya in East Africa. I enjoyed the work, and the salary was slightly better than at the YWCA. I also had a proper office, where I was put in charge of secretarial and clerical matters. The company was very impressed with what I did, and offered me another posting in Dar es Salaam in Tanzania, with better pay and as one of their executive directors. I turned it down, not feeling quite ready for that type of responsibility.

In September 1984 I discovered I was pregnant. However,

I was working so hard, often staying after hours in the office, and I had a miscarriage. Jimmy, for his part, did not feel ready for the responsibility of being a father. We were both twenty-seven. Despite that, before I had had the miscarriage, I'd already decided to go ahead and have the child on my own, without any support from him. When the miscarriage came, it was at the office, and was extremely painful. I think that emotionally, too, I was not prepared for being a mother.

In November my visa had almost expired, and instead of applying for an extension I decided to go back to Nigeria for three months, and reapply from there. I left at the end of the month. Jimmy and I decided that I could be away for three months, which gave me ample time to visit family and friends. I ended up staying for eight months, with Africonsult offering to keep my job open. I left my address and phone number in Nigeria with them, in case they needed me.

I took three very big suitcases, travelling first to Liverpool, from where I shipped my goods on the *River Jimini*. My suitcases went free of charge, and were filled with shoes, bags and clothes for resale in Nigeria. When I got to Nigeria I travelled to Lagos and Kogi State. I collected my cases from Lagos, and took very little time in disposing of all my goods. Some people bought from me on credit, and where I was not able to collect from these debtors, I made a loss. For the whole eight months that I was there, repeated efforts to collect these debts met with very little success. Still, I had Jimmy to think about, and also my job at Africonsult – who were now saying that if I didn't come back soon they would employ someone else. I kept telling them to be patient.

Jimmy moved out of his house in Park Royal to a friend's in Willesden Green, North London. He telephoned me to say that if I didn't come back soon he would have to get a new girlfriend. I wasn't going to respond to his threats so I took my time getting back. In any case, I was having a difficult time in Nigeria, having run out of money. I went to see some of my old boyfriends and asked if I could work in their offices, but nothing turned up. In the end I managed to save enough to buy a single ticket to London, though not before thinking I wouldn't make it back at all.

My family and friends were happy to see me, but none of them was able to give me money – though they did help me to round up my debtors. In due course I faced the problem head-on, and decided, come what may, on a return to England. I knew it wasn't going to be easy. The mistake I made was to travel with very little money, and no proper arrangement as to where I might stay. However, I knew I had a very strong personality, and was one of life's survivors. If necessary, Jimmy and I could rent somewhere, though I little knew of the difficulties and the very hard times that lay ahead.

I arrived in London on the afternoon of 5 August 1985, a Saturday. I was met at Heathrow Airport by Jimmy and his friend Simon Woodman, who had come to collect me. I was pleased and happy to see them.

Jimmy and Simon took me to a friend's house, whom we referred to as Aunty. As of this moment accommodation was a problem as I discovered from Jimmy that I could not stay with him. The rental contract he had signed had run out, and he himself was sharing with a friend at Willeseden Green, in north London. I stayed with Aunty for a few days and she secured me a room in another lady's flat, who was letting a room. This was in Kingsbury, also north London. I cannot remember precisely how much I paid for this, but she increased the rent after a while. My landlady laid down the rules. In particular, and this was made clear from the beginning, she did not want my boyfriend staying overnight. During the day, when she was out at work, I would tidy up the flat, as the whole place was very unkempt. She was happy with me doing this.

Jimmy came to see me during the afternoons before I started work. I cooked for him at lunchtime and sometimes we would make love in the afternoon – what a good life this was, I thought. Then he would eat and go back to work. This went on for a month or two before I started job hunting. I went back to my old job at the YWCA, where there was a vacancy. Now, however, I worked in a different department with a different boss. He was called John Skiffington. My salary was slightly higher and I had more responsibility, but most of the time I left the office a little earlier than it closed, because my boss had a soft spot for me.

I worked there until I got pregnant with what would be my first child. I was sacked by the managing director, Mrs Bellington, as it was leaked to her that I had been pregnant before I joined the organisation – I was there less than six months. I was devastated. This was only a few days before the office Christmas party. She called me to her office and explained to me why she had to terminate my appointment, and that I could re-apply for work after the delivery of my baby. That Christmas was one mixed with happiness, joy and sadness, for myself and Jimmy, and also the beginning of hardship and many more problems coming our way.

Meanwhile, my landlady increased the rent, so I had no alternative but to move out.

Jimmy spoke with his friend Simon, to see if I could share his flat in Fulham while I paid him minimal expenses, but he gladly let me stay rent-free. I was with him for a few weeks, until I secured accommodation in East Dulwich, in south-east London. I was almost five months' pregnant.

In January 1986, I rented a room and parlour from a landlord, a Nigerian man called Mr Julius Adewumi. This was in Lordship Lane in East Dulwich. Mr Julius Adewumi was a peculiar and strange man, who lived on his own except for a couple of student tenants in the house. I noticed this only after I had negotiated my rent. At first, he was not observant enough to see that I was pregnant, and I didn't tell him. I was not big in my pregnancy, in fact I was very small, and in less than a week after I moved into the house, he made advances towards me, and said that he would not like a boyfriend to visit me. I explained to him that I did have a boyfriend, and pointed out I had already introduced Jimmy to him when he helped me move into the house. I also told Mr Julius Adewumi that I was pregnant. He was furious and said he did not want a pregnant woman in his house, but luckily for me a contract had been signed, so he couldn't get rid of me until the contract expired.

My boyfriend visited me regularly and sometimes stayed the weekend. Mr Julius Adewumi and I had arguments all the time. As I said, he was a strange man. He would put his ear against the door of my bedroom, and he peeped through the keyhole. I know this because I opened the door on three separate occasions and caught him unawares. He was interested in any conversation between Jimmy and me, and perhaps he was watching our activities too. One other habit he had was to visit the kitchen at night when everyone was asleep, or when he came back late from work, or during the day when all his tenants were out of the house, and he would help himself to the cooked meals in the fridge I had prepared for myself – soups or stews. He also purloined uncooked food that we stored in the kitchen cupboards.

I asked the other tenants in the house if they had taken any of these items, and they all said no – actually some of their provisions were missing too. I confronted Mr Julius Adewumi about this, and this resulted in another big argument, but finally I caught him red-handed. He admitted to his theft and apologised, but he continued to do it.

Before the end of January 1986 Jimmy travelled to Jamaica, in the West Indies, for four to six weeks on a working holiday. He asked me if I wanted to go with him, but I said no – I was not in a fit state to travel as I was still having morning sickness. Even more pressing, I wanted to sort myself out in England and get ready for the birth of my baby. I missed him when he went and all I was left with was his friends, and of course Mr Julius Adewumi. He had already heard our conversations through the closed door, and so knew where Jimmy had gone. It gave him the opportunity to make life more difficult for me. When Jimmy was around he defended me, but of course he was not here now. The arguments went on, and sometimes Mr Julius Adewumi would turn off the gas supply so that I was unable to cook. He would switch it on again when the other tenants needed it, but scenes like this went on for some time. I told him that if I did not have all my rights as a tenant, I would not pay him that week's rent, or for any weeks that he disconnected the gas. He did not like that, so I threatened to report him to the law, and withheld two weeks' rent.

On one particular occasion, one evening, I came back from my shopping and went to use the bathroom, where I discovered that all my toiletries had been misplaced and that my Clinique soap bar had been used and almost cut into two. I was furious. I asked one of the girls if she had used it and she said no, though she'd seen Mr Julius Adewumi leave the bathroom five minutes before I got in. I confronted him angrily, asking him why he had to do such a thing, and told him how expensive the soap was. The next thing I knew he punched me so hard in the face, I almost passed out. He kept on punching me everywhere, though I barred my stomach with my hands, desperate to save my baby. I was in such pain and I was dizzy. This was a freezing February night. My room was dark and cold, as was the whole house because Mr Julius Adewumi had turned off the electricity and all the heating with it, regardless of everyone else. They all saw what had happened – even a man who was his guest for one night, who watched and did nothing while I was being punched.

I managed to stay rested in my room until about 11.30 p.m., when I staggered to the nearest police station. I made a complaint and the police asked me if I needed to go to hospital to check if my baby was all right. I told them I was fine. Policemen followed me to the house and questioned and took evidence from Mr Julius Adewumi. He denied most of what I said, and the policemen left me to come back the following day. I was frightened to sleep in the house that night, and I knew I had to take some sort of action to protect my well-being. At midnight I went to the

Town Hall in Peckham, to lay my case before the local authorities. I was declared homeless by Social Services, as luckily there were a few people on night duty. I filled in various forms, showed them the evidence from the police and evidence of bruises on my body. I was taken to the nearest bed-and-breakfast hotel used by Social Services, and did not go back to my flat in Lordship Lane that night. It was about 2.30 a.m. when I finally got to the Dome Hotel. I went to bed in a lot of pain, and hardly slept. In the morning I had to report to various organisations – Social Services and Social Security among them – and I also had to report to the police station. I managed to do all that, but I was soon exhausted and feeling disorientated. The process continued for a good while until I had all the benefits I was entitled to, and all my rights to accommodation were arranged. I was a high priority on the waiting list in the local authority's housing scheme.

It was now the end of February 1986, and when Jimmy came back from Jamaica he was devastated at all that had happened to me. He blamed himself for leaving me behind but I quickly assured him that that was not the case. He went along with me to the Social Security office to let them know that he was the father of my unborn baby, and asked if he could be allowed to move in with me at the hotel. He was told no. He visited me as often as he could. He was with me virtually all day every day. The police visited Mr Julius Adewumi once more and he assured them that I would be safe with him when I collected the rest of my belongings from his house. Nevertheless, I asked for police protection when Jimmy and I and his friends went with a van to pick everything up. Thank God I did that, because he was ready to attack me again, thinking I had come alone. When he saw the policemen with me he quickly changed his tone.

I was in the Dome Hotel for two months, and then disaster happened. I was secretly cooking in my bedroom one evening at about 5 p.m., as one was not allowed to use the kitchen. I was using a small gas-ring cooker I had bought the week previously. I didn't know it had a fault. It blew up and smoke billowed out. The hotel manager telephoned my room from the reception area and reminded me of the rules about cooking. I panicked and denied any wrongdoing, and tried to hide the cooker and the food. However, everything in the room went up in flames, and within a few minutes the whole upstairs of the hotel was ablaze. We were evacuated and the fire brigade was called. This again was at night. All my property, clothes, electronic equipment – my radio, television and my stereo player – as well other people's property next door to me were destroyed. I had only the dress that I was wearing.

We were taken to the nearby King's College Hospital in Camberwell for examination. Almost all the people at the hotel were pregnant women or families with children, but I thank my lucky stars that everybody examined was passed fit. There were no casualties, and everyone was sympathetic towards me. That was another experience in my life I would always remember. The police were once again called in and since we were next to the Town Hall, Social Services came and managed to relocate us all, in the early hours of the morning, to another hotel in Elephant and Castle. Insurance was claimed and the Dome Hotel was rebuilt, looking much nicer and bigger. Everyone also claimed compensation for the possessions they'd lost, which was all mentioned in the local newspaper at the time.

At the hotel in Elephant and Castle I learnt my lesson. I never cooked at all in the hotel. It was a bigger place and had a guest dining area, which was more convenient and comfortable. Jimmy this time was allowed to move in with me, and I started attending my antenatal clinic at King's College Hospital. I was keeping well but I was worn out. In May 1986, the local council gave me a flat in Peckham, southeast London. It was given to me in my name because Jimmy and I were not married at the time. Jimmy moved in with me straightaway.

We stayed in love with each other as we prepared for the birth of our baby, which arrived in June 1986.

Epilogue

I am currently working on my second book. This is a continuation of my life story, and follows on directly from the events described above. Due to the problems I encountered socially and all the obstacles that came my way, and having gone through one disaster after another, I suffered from what started as post-natal depression, and developed into severe depression for many years. This was an illness I finally overcame. Jimmy and I got married and had two children. In the past nineteen years, since I have been in England, my life has changed so much. I coped with issues of inter-racial marriage and the problems this threw up.

I will be telling the story of the break-up of my marriage and having to cope with two children as a single mother in my next book. I went to college to train as a professional cook, and I now work part-time in that line. I am also now in another relationship.

These are friends who have passed away since the completion of this book:

Bosede Koledade
Mode Orimolade
Olajmoke Ogundalu
Dolapo Ebeizua

Miss Ogwogwo

May their souls rest in perfect peace.